Zen has proved one of the most popular forms of Buddhism for Western minds. Zen has no God, nor dogma of any kind. It is a way of perceiving, thinking, acting and being. With its unique methods of meditation, questioning, intuition and artistic cultivation, Zen can bring an amazing degree of spiritual, emotional and mental poise and it is possible to attain a deep awareness of one's self, of nature and the world.

'Lively, lucid book by eminent Buddhist.'

The Sunday Times

'He presents a very comprehensive idea of Zen in all its aspects.'

World Buddhism

'The process of Zen is a leap from thinking to knowing . . . Christmas Humphreys expounds with great clarity an often misinterpreted way of life.'

The Bookman

By the same author

THE BUDDHIST WAY OF LIFE
EXPLORING BUDDHISM
A WESTERN APPROACH TO ZEN

ZEN BUDDHISM

Christmas Humphreys

DIAMOND
BOOKS

This edition published 1996 by
Diamond Books
77-85 Fulham Palace Road
Hammersmith, London W6 8JB

First published in Great Britain by William Heinemann Ltd, 1949
Reprinted by George Allen & Unwin 1957, 1958
First published in paperback 1961
First published in Uwin Paperbacks 1976
First published as Mandala Edition 1984

ISBN 0 261 66933 8

Printed in Great Britain

For Hasuko

Contents

Preface

Zen is the essence and value of life, that which makes life worth living. Being that which uses and discards all forms, whether of thought, words or material substance, it cannot be described in terms of form. As Taoism, the godmother of Zen, declared of Tao, "The Tao that can be described is not the eternal Tao."

Yet "to get it across" (a most thought-provoking phrase) some form is necessary, and in a book which is not merely about Zen, but which attempts to transfer the life of Zen to the receptive reader, a style must be devised to the occasion. To this end I have fashioned a mixture of the flippant and the deadly serious, the rational and the irrational, or, as Zen would put it, super-rational. It leads the reader's mind to the precipice which lies between the highest thought and the humblest truth and then, by a jerk or joke, tries to push it over. It tries to unite the far and near, the pseudo-holy ideal and the no less holy umbrella-stand. As Ruysbroeck said, "You are as holy as you will be," and in Zen all things are as holy as you make them, being in themselves neither divine nor blush-producing, but precisely what they are. When all is Mind, says Zen, why divide into the compartments of space and time the all-here and the only now? The style of this book, then, is deliberate. If it holds the reader to the task in hand it is good: if not, it is not so good, for the reader.

I do not apologise for being occasionally personal, in opinion or the record of experience, for one cannot speak of the deeps of Zen like a salesman selling a car. Nor do I regret occasional repetition. The young are advised in my profession to say a thing once to a judge, twice to a bench of magistrates, and three times to a jury. This is often too polite to the judge.

My liberal use of quotations has three causes. I wish to show that others, widely scattered in time and space, hold views which, however strange, are those now being expressed, and the writers quoted generally say what I wish to say in far better words than my own. Thirdly, their voices vary the attack, as one might say, on the citadel of the reader's mind. The most quoted author is, of course, Professor D. T. Suzuki of Japan, for, as a glance at the Bibliography will show, his books, booklets and articles on Zen provide at least three quarters of all that has yet been written on the subject in English, and much that others have written in the last twenty years is only a paraphrase of his material. To him must be rendered thanks, by all who understand the profound importance of gratitude, for our Western knowledge of Zen.

My reasons for writing this book are, first, that the interest in Zen is rapidly rising, and although the Buddhist Society, with the help of Rider and Co., are now reprinting Dr. Suzuki's Collected Works on Zen, there is need for a book which attempts to collate this eastern way of attainment with our western approach to the same experience. Alan Watts' little book, *The Spirit of Zen*, though brilliant, only whets the appetite; W. J. Gabb's *Beyond the Intellect*, even though fortified by his later lectures, soon, I hope, to be published as *Studies in Zen Buddhism*,[1] is too subjective to cover the intellectual field. But if these are the reasons for the book, the cause is otherwise, and quite irrational. I wrote it as one writes a poem—because it came.

My qualifications are small. I studied the works of Dr. Suzuki as they appeared; I am editing his Collected Works, and in the course of this tremendous task have re-read the whole of them. I spent seven months in Japan in 1946, and much of this time at the feet of the Master; I have tried to live Zen. But I am not a master of Zen, not even a pupil of one, and the average Zen master, were he to read this book, would probably roar with laughter and put it to useful purposes. But being a poet and not a philosopher, and therefore possessing the power which the poet shares with the child and all great men, of "sitting loose to life" and adding labels to nothing, I offer the fruits of my own experience to those in search of them.

The book should be Zen, but, being in words, it must still be about it. After all, "He who knows does not speak; he who speaks does not know," as the *Tao Te Ching* points out: and as Alan Watts quite rightly says, "In writing about Zen there are two extremes to be avoided: the one to define and explain so little that the reader is completely bewildered, and the other to define and explain so much that the reader thinks he understands Zen!"[2] For one does not understand Zen, any more than one understands breathing or walking. The wise man breathes, and walks on.

[1] This material has in fact been published by the Buddhist Society in 1956 as *The Goose is Out*.
[2] *The Spirit of Zen*, p. 131.

It is a difficult book. As Leonardo da Vinci said, "The line that is straightest offers most resistance."[1] It is also largely nonsense, and the original title of the book was in fact *What nonsense! An Enquiry into Zen Buddhism.* But with such a title it might be classified on the bookstalls with the usual forms of nonsense, and those who bought it as such might be cross to find super-sense inside it.

Professor J. B. Pratt relates that when he first contacted Zen he found it "unspeakably queer". So it is, deliciously so, for though we know about nonsense and much about sense, when we rise still higher to what is nonsense because it is super-sense we are truly through the Looking-Glass, and the fun begins, and with it the battle and the joy thereof. In terms of this classification, the book is written at the level of sense, but retires at times into nonsense in order the better to leap into non-sense, or the light of Zen. Please read it as such.

American readers will note that the book was serialised in the *Theosophical Forum*, the Journal of the Theosophical Society, Covina, California, edited by Colonel Arthur L. Conger.

I thank herewith Dr. Suzuki, who gave us Zen, and R. H. Blyth, whose sixteen years in Korea have taught him a world of Zen from which I have, with the help of his *Zen in English Literature and Oriental Classics,* picked such crumbs as I may. I am grateful to Alan Watts for his brilliant words on Zen, and to that brave man W. J. Gabb, who, in his lectures to the Buddhist Society, London, revealed so much of his Zen experience. I am grateful to those who have tried to fair-copy my original typing and temperamental corrections; to my wife, who allowed me to walk in a dazzle of Zen while I bumped into the furniture; to those who corrected the proofs and then, to my surprise and shattered feelings, asked me what the book was all about. The illustrations are mostly from my own collection of photographs and works of art; the wrapper and end-plates are by Hasuko, who in private life is my wife, and manager, and friend.

CHRISTMAS HUMPHREYS

St. John's Wood.
February, 1949.

[1] Leonardo da Vinci's Notebooks, McCURDY. p. 58.

Preface to the Mandala Edition

Much has happened in the field of Zen since the publication of this account of the Zen School of Buddhism in 1949.

The word itself has acquired three different meanings. As ZEN it is rightly equated with Reality, the Absolute, the Void, or what the Buddha called "the Unborn, Unoriginated, Unformed". As such it is a postulate beyond argument or proof, the Beyond without which the field of relativity is meaningless. The Zen school, however, is a matter of history and examination. Zen, its special subject, is a term for awareness beyond the intellect but as such is a legitimate subject for teaching and discussion. As prostituted in the United States and elsewhere as "Beat Zen" it is nonsense beyond the range of reason and of any spiritual worth.

Meanwhile, much has been written on the subject by responsible students. Its metaphysical background, "the Wisdom that has gone beyond" of the Prajnaparamita literature, has been deeply studied. Sayings of masters have been newly collated and translated, and we now have the recorded experience of students who have lived in Zen monasteries, and one Westerner at least who, on achieving his *inka* as a Roshi of the Rinzai school, teaches in the West. Japanese Roshis have increasingly visited Europe. More and more seekers from Europe and the U.S. have spent substantial periods of time in Zen monasteries in Japan and returned to record their experience.

The effect of these newly established lines of communication is difficult to assess, but it may have contributed to the wakening of the hitherto ignored faculty of the intuition present in every human mind. As a power of direct knowledge beyond the limitations of reasoning it is increasingly recognised, not only in psychology and religion but as a new working factor in the field of science by which the mind can "know" beyond the range of intellectual proof.

This new awareness is the sole subject of Zen Buddhism, as founded in China by Bodhidharma as Ch'an and carried to Japan as Zen. The present work may therefore be usefully studied as the basis for all further enquiry.

Note: When the Buddhist Society began to import the Sutra of Hui Neng from China, before the war, the name appeared as Wei Lang, this being the Cantonese dialect version used by the translator, Mr. Wong Mou-Lam. Later the standard version was adopted, and all references in the text and bibliography to Wei Lang should be read as Hui Neng.

Chapter 1

Beyond the Intellect

Buddhism is the religion-philosophy built up round the Teaching of Gotama, the Buddha. Zen Buddhism is a sect of the Mahayana, the Northern School of Buddhism. *Zen*, a corruption of the Chinese *Ch'an*, which is in turn a corruption of the Sanskrit word, *Dhyâna,* is a Japanese term for that Wisdom-Power-Compassion which lies beyond all words, and cannot be confined in the largest "ism". It is the Light in the darkness of *avidyâ*, Ignorance, the Life within all changing, perishable forms. It is the meaning in circumstance. It is at once the Life, the Truth, and the Way.

This Light or Wisdom—and who shall bind awareness in a word?—is the goal of mysticism and the subject matter of all religions. All alike are concerned with an Ultimate which lies beyond change and the sway of the "opposites"; all seek or claim to seek, to KNOW. Zen, however, using the term as a means to achieve this plane of consciousness, is unique. Zen Buddhism, to the extent that it is a form of Buddhism, may be compared with other attempts to erect a ladder from the unreal to the Real; but Zen, as the direct, im-mediate, "sudden" path to Awareness is, in the history and present state of spiritual experience, unique. It eschews the machinery of philosophy, the mediation of religion, and the practical "devices" of ritual and magic. It climbs, with empty hands, from the level of "usual life" to the heights of spiritual awareness. The effort is terrific; the results are commensurate. The whole process takes place within the mind, which, being part of All-Mind, is already in a sense enlightened. For, as Patriarch Hui-neng declared in one of the greatest of Zen Scriptures,

"the Essence of Mind is intrinsically pure; to meditate means to realise inwardly the imperturbability of the Essence of Mind."[1]

Zen is at once the knower and the known. It is also the factor

[1] *The Sutra of Wei Lang* (Hui-neng), 52.

which unites the two in one. It is a way to Truth and not facts about Truth. As Dr. Suzuki puts it, "When we think we know something, there is something we do not know." For there is still an antithesis, the known and the knower, and Zen seeks that which lies beyond antitheses, however subtle.

"If science surveys the objective world, and philosophy unravels intricacies of logic, Buddhism dives into the very abyss of being, and tells us in the directest possible manner all it sees under the surface."[1]

Strictly speaking, however, Zen is incommunicable. Even as "The Tao that can be expressed is not the Eternal Tao", so Zen translated into the terms and apparatus of the intellect is not true Zen. There is therefore an inevitable distinction between Zen and the forms of Zen, between expressions *of* Zen, and facts *about* Zen, but it is the aim of Zen Buddhists to reduce to a minimum these bridges between the mind and its essential purity and to achieve, with the minimum delay, the direct, im-mediate fusion of subject-object, the seeker and the sought, the Lover, the Beloved and the power of Love.

The "transmission" of Zen is a matter of prime difficulty. Creations of the intellect, such as philosophy or mathematics, can be conveyed from mind to mind with tolerable ease, for the bridge between is on the same plane as the matter to be conveyed. Zen, however, is *ex hypothesi* beyond the intellect, and the coins of intellectual usage, such as words and diagrams, have no validity.

"Intuitionalism requires pointers more than ideas to express itself, and these pointers are enigmatic and non-rational. They are shy of intellectual interpretation. They have a decided aversion towards circumlocution. They do not repeat, and brevity is their essence. They are like flashes of lightning. While your eyes blink they are gone."[2]

All that a teacher can do, therefore, is to speak, write, paint or act in such a way as to arouse and address the faculty of direct knowledge, which is known in the East as Buddhi, and in the West as the intuition. Intuition, the awakening of which Dr. Suzuki describes as "the unfolding of a new world hitherto unperceived in the confusion of a dualistically-trained mind", is "man's highest

[1] *Essays in Zen Buddhism*, SUZUKI, III, 69.
[2] *Buddhism in the Life and Thought of Japan*, SUZUKI, p. 25.

faculty of perception, a kind of spiritual illumination which manifests only when the thought and sense-impressions of personal life have been brought into silence".

In re-reading some sixty books and articles on Zen before beginning this book, I was struck once again with the profound difference between the various writers' plane of inspiration. Some, notably Dr. and Mrs. Suzuki, Alan Watts, R. H. Blyth and Victor Reinaecker, write from the intuitive level; others, the vast majority, though they may have attained considerable standing in the world of thought, still write with the intellect. The same distinction may be found in the Scriptures of all religions. Those used by the followers of Zen, however, have the same intuitive quality and, as it were, ring in the mind the bell of immediate, glad acceptance. The *Lankâvatâra Sûtra,* the *Diamond Sutra,* the *Sutra of Wci Lang* (Hui-neng) and *The Voice of the Silence* speak from and therefore to the intuition, and the *sumiye* art of Chinese painting and the Japanese *haiku,* or short poem, have the same effect. Lesser writers, painters and poets "explain", and Zen can no more be explained than a joke. You see it or you don't. There is no compromise.

Zen belongs to the intuitive plane. It is therefore beyond discussion, and beyond the sway of the "opposites" by which all description and argument are carried on. It must therefore be understood on its own plane or not at all, for the intellect can never understand or assimilate spiritual facts. A rose may be torn in pieces, and each particle analysed in the laboratory; no scientist will find therein the beauty of the rose. "Intellect", as Dr. C. G. Jung points out in his *Secret of the Golden Flower,* "does in fact violate the soul when it tries to possess itself of the heritage of the spirit" (p. 81). Those, therefore, who have not developed intuition to the point where it may be used for the understanding of Zen are implored to read no further. It is useless to attempt to drag Zen down to the intellectual plane. The intellect may argue and debate; it may learn and teach a vast amount about almost anything; it can never KNOW. Those who attempt to study it with the mind by which they approach philosophy, psychology or business affairs will either be intensely annoyed or exceedingly amused, and in either case will thereby exhibit nothing but their own insufficiency. Climb, I beg of you, to the abode of Zen, or leave it in the peace in which it abides until such time as, failing to find content elsewhere, you climb to your heritage.

Zen is a matter of experience. This statement, simple to express, is all that can usefully be said. The rest is silence, and a finger pointing the way. But the faculty of direct experience, naked, direct experience, stripped of the mediating factors of thought, emotion, ritual or the convenient invention which men call God, is comparatively rare, and brave is the heart which knows it. Wherefore let us examine the instrument by which we achieve experience, but first let us look at the instrument by which, all day and every day, we are forced to be satisfied with the next best thing.

What is the intellect? Maeterlinck in *The Life of the White Ant* calls it "the quality which enables us to comprehend at last that all is incomprehensible". It is, however, of more use than that. It is, indeed, an essential tool in the hands of a developed man. By it alone he climbs beyond the power of merely sensuous reaction and the sway of his desires. By it alone he compares, selects and evaluates in terms of an ever receding ideal. All this is obvious, but its limitations should be no less obvious. R. H. Blyth has given them as three. First, he says, "it usurps the function of religion in supposing that it can understand life. The intellect can understand intellectual things; life can understand living things. But they cannot understand each other, so long as they are apart." Secondly, he says, "it usurps the function of poetry when it replaces the imagination, the compassion, of the poet." For the poet, being in close and constant touch with life itself, has still the gift of wonder.

"Sell your cleverness and buy bewilderment:
Cleverness is mere opinion, bewilderment is intuition."[1]

Lastly, says Mr. Blyth, in his *Zen in English Literature*—the finest book yet written on the subject—"the intellect is guilty of constructing dogmas, systems of philosophy which imprison the mind until it mopes like a monkey in a cage." (pp. 171 *et seq*). Great though its uses are, therefore, it would seem that the intellect, so far as the search for Truth is concerned, exists but to lead us to the point where it may be superseded. As Aldous Huxley says:

"In the last analysis the use and purpose of reason is to create the internal and external conditions favourable to its own transfigura-

[1] *Jalal-uddin Rumi.*

tion by and into spirit. It is the lamp by which it finds the way to go beyond itself."[1]

The intellect is admittedly the instrument of proof, but in my experience nothing worth proving can be proved, and the intuition needs no proof by the intellect; it KNOWS. Moreover, the field of the intellect is severely limited in range. In the words of Dr. Kenneth Walker:

"It is like the police constable's bull's-eye lantern that concentrates illumination on one particular spot, so that we can take note of a particular object which at that moment has a particular significance for us. For the practical purposes of living the intellect is an excellent contrivance, but as a means of revealing 'the whole' it is useless as the constable's bull's-eye lantern in revealing the world."[2]

There is a more serious limitation which amounts to a defect. The intellect raises far more problems than it solves and leaves the heart disquieted. As Dr. Suzuki points out,

"it upsets the blissful peace of ignorance, and yet it does not restore the former state of things by offering something else. ... It is not final, it waits for something higher than itself for the solution of all the questions it will raise regardless of consequences."[3]

How, then, does it work, this faculty of the mind which men so highly prize and far too lightly claim to be infallible? The answer is, by the interaction of the opposites. Think of it. If I were asked where I live I might reply: in a semi-detached Regency house of yellow brick in St. John's Wood, London. I have described the house by choosing from an indefinite list of pairs of opposite attributes. I have, for example, explained that it is *not* a modern, detached (or unattached) grey stone house in the country. In the same way I could describe a speech as having been given briefly, dramatically, to the point, and should be saying thereby that it was *not* given tediously, flatly and full of irrelevance. The police description of a wanted man gives all the details as a series of selected opposites, and all conversation is carried on in the same way. Objective descriptions are built up by selections of epithets

[1] *The Perennial Philosophy*, p. 163.
[2] *Diagnosis of Man*, p. 118.
[3] *Essays in Zen Buddhism*, I, 6.

about things; subjective reactions centre about the ideas thus brought to birth in the mind. In the same way, emotional values depend on the complementary forces of like and dislike, attraction and repulsion. But these values are later found to be as false as those of the intellect, which speaks of the true and the untrue. Even while using these endless pairs of opposing attributes we know that sooner or later they will be proved untrue. As R. H. Blyth most forcefully puts it,

"To God, a man is the same on a chamber-pot or a throne. All men are naked under their clothes. A tiger seems a nobler animal than a bed-bug. There seem to be vessels of honour and vessels of dishonour, and in this short life we can hardly escape this feeling, but at the back of our minds, in the bottom of our hearts, there must be the full realisation that there is no difference between birth and death, the entrance and the exit, good morning and good night, the dining-room and the lavatory."[1]

The opposites are endless, for they reproduce each other.

"When all in the world understand beauty to exist, then ugliness exists. When all understand goodness to be good, then evil exists. Thus existence suggests non-existence; easy gives rise to difficult. Short is derived from long by comparison ... after follows before."[2]

And they fight.

"When thought is divided dualistically, it seeks to favour one at the cost of the other, but as dualism is the very condition of thought, it is impossible for thought to rise above its own condition."

So the fight goes on, the two contestants failing to observe that as they are but modes of one another there can be neither victory nor defeat.

Consider now the intuition, the faculty beyond the sway of the opposites, which moves on the plane of direct experience. Our knowledge is derived through one of two faculties, the senses and the intuition. Both are direct. But whereas the senses only give us knowledge of the things of the physical plane, the intuition enlightens us at its own level. In the words of Plotinus, "It is absolute knowledge founded on the identity of the mind knowing

[1] *Zen in English Literature*, p. 256.
[2] *The Tao Te Ching*, Chap. 2.

with the object known." It KNOWS with an inner certainty quite maddening to the mind which, with intellectual arguments, dares to disagree. True, the use of the new-found instrument is in no way under control. These flashes of true understanding come, or they do not. They may be sought, but for a long while they are beyond command. Only the constant use of the newly awakened faculty, testing each new "certainty" in the light of reason and previous experience, will enable the power, as a muscle wisely used, to grow.

All men have this faculty, but few develop it consciously. It is the summit of a pyramid of growth and development. There is, in the words of Aldous Huxley, "a hierarchy of the real. The manifold world of our everyday experience is real with a relative reality that is, on its own level, unquestionable; but this relative reality has its being within and because of the absolute Reality which, on account of the incommensurable otherness of its eternal nature, we can never hope to describe, even though it is possible for us directly to apprehend it."[1]

Viewing the complex entity of the self in terms of its ascending powers we have, beyond the senses, the emotions, and beyond them the workaday practical mind. This analytic, concrete mind is sooner or later used by a higher faculty, the abstract and synthetic mind. This, in Buddhist philosophy, creates the man as we know him. As the most famous of all Buddhist Scriptures has it:

"All that we are is the result of what we have thought; it is compounded of our thoughts, made up of our thoughts."[2]

Between the lower and the higher aspects of the mind is a bridge in the crossing of which the faculty of Buddhi, the intuition, begins to illumine the intellect. The type of thought is immaterial, so that it be high, reaching ever for the abstract and impersonal ultimates wherein true wisdom dwells. On such a plane the musician, the mathematician, the philosopher and the mystic find they are walking and working side by side. Here self begins to doubt itself, and the vast sweep of the impersonal commands the attention of the awakening mind. Yet there is no severance between the two aspects of the mind, however fierce the tension. The lower clings to the earth, the higher strives for the splendour of the windy sky. The two are one, and sooner or later are seen as such. Dr. Jung has

[1] *The Perennial Philosophy*, p. 42.
[2] *Dhammapada*, Verse I.

enriched our understanding of the mind with a diagram of its main
"pairs of opposites". All men, he says, are predominantly
intellectual or emotional, and all—and this is the more exciting
pair—predominantly more intuitive or sensuous. Note the
opposites, how spirit and matter reflect into each other, and are
modes of one another on their respective planes. Here is new
meaning for the immortal phrase in *The Voice of the Silence*:

"Avert thy face from world deceptions: mistrust the senses; they
are false. But within thy body—the shrine of thy sensations—seek
in the Impersonal for the 'Eternal Man'; and having sought him
out, look inward: thou art Buddha."

Such is the intellect, the field of the Opposites. Such is the
intuition, where every two is One. Zen is the path, the direct,
unswerving path, which leads beyond the intellect.

At an early stage of thought we appreciate that the opposites
must sooner or later be reconciled. But how? It seems that the
answers are no more than five. We can choose between the
opposites, and cleave to the one of our choice. This leaves the
world in an endless dualism, with all the tension, strife and
suffering which dualism entails. We may clothe our decision in the
mantle of logic, and glibly speak of an absolute affirmation of all
experience; it will not avail, for if this be true, we can equally
absolutely deny. We can, secondly, unite them, and say that black
is white and white is black. But this is such nonsense to the rational
mind that it is used in Zen to break up the limitations of conceptual
thought, and free the student from his concept-ridden mind. It has
its value, but not as a means of solving the opposites; rather it can
be used to develop the intuition which can alone transcend them.
Here is one of the most famous sayings in Zen:

"Empty-handed I go, and behold, the spade is in my hand;
I walk on foot, yet on the back of an ox am I riding,
When I pass over the bridge
Lo, the water floweth not; it is the bridge doth flow."

Zen Masters will use this method of intriguing, and even
annoying, the mind, indefinitely. Basho, a Korean monk of the
ninth century, once delivered a sermon the whole of which ran, "If
you have a staff I will give you one; if not, I will take it away." Or
again, Joshu, a famous Zen Master, when asked, "When a man
comes to you with nothing, what would you advise?", replied

without hesitation, "Throw it away!" All this, however, is an appeal to the intuition, and no solution on their own plane of the tension of the opposites.

One can compromise. But the Buddhist "Middle Way" is no mere compromise. As a reasonable middle way between the extremes of asceticism and self-indulgence it may, though unfairly, be described as compromise, but as between the rival claims of what the individual believes to be right and wrong there is here no teaching of "a little of each and not too much of either". Grey is a poor substitute for a decision about black or white. Nor is compromise a solution to the problem on the mental plane. For here is a third factor which is not even a higher third. Instead of the antithesis of black and white we now have black, grey and white, and presumably varieties of grey. Compromise may palliate the tension of the opposites. It cannot solve the antithesis.

A better solution is to seek a synthesis *above* the opposing pairs. "Truth lies *beyond* the extremes, not in the middle; is beyond good and evil, not partly both."[1] Above good and evil is Good; above the ugly and the beautiful is Beauty; above the true and the untrue lies the True. Once a glimpse of this state of affairs is experienced, and this is the operative word, a new truth dawns in the awakening consciousness. It is that the opposition from which we seek to escape never in fact existed. In the "higher third" of the triangle we do not identify the opposites. Rather do we realise that there never existed any opposing terms.

"Identification presupposes original opposition of two terms, subject and object, but the truth is that from the very first there are no two opposing terms whose identification is to be achieved by Zen. ... The aim of Zen is to restore the experience of original inseparability, which means, to restore the original state of purity and transparency."[2]

In other words, to find and function in "the Essence of Mind which is intrinsically pure".

This viewpoint involves the transference of the point of habitual consciousness.

"Only the truly intelligent understand this principle of the identity of all things. They do not view things as apprehended by

[1] *Zen in English Literature*, BLYTH, p. 84.
[2] *Zen Buddhism and its Influence on Japanese Culture*, SUZUKI, p. 233.

themselves, subjectively, but transfer themselves into the position of the things viewed. And viewing them thus they are able to comprehend them, nay, to master them;—and he who can master them is near. So it is that to place oneself in subjective relation with externals, without consciousness of their objectivity,—this is TAO."[1]

It is also Zen, and the great Taoist sage illustrated his theme with a typically Chinese parallel.

"To wear out one's intellect in an obstinate adherence to the individuality of things, not recognising the fact that all things are ONE,—this is called *Three in the Morning*."

Asked what he meant by Three in the Morning, the Master replied:

"A keeper of monkeys said with regard to their ration of chestnuts that each monkey was to have three in the morning and four at night. But at this the monkeys were very angry, so the keeper said they might have four in the morning and three at night, with which arrangement they were all well pleased. The actual number of chestnuts remained the same, but there was an adaptation to the likes and dislikes of those concerned. Such is the principle of putting oneself into subjective relation with externals."

This Chinese habit of illustrating a spiritual principle with an almost flippant story is deliberate, for it rouses the intuition, to which it is addressed, without calling into the play the slow machinery of conceptual thought which it is the principal purpose of the "sudden" school to avoid.

This point of view produces tolerance, for good and evil in the world of the opposites have equal value, or none. It broadens the sympathies, for the whole of manifestation, not an arbitrary half, is experienced. It emphasises that all alike is a matter of experience; all life becomes the "soul's gymnasium". We have no enemies thereafter, for all can teach us something, and the most unexpected teacher is an excellent friend.

But this is not the end. "If all is reduced to the One, to what is the One reduced?" Such is a famous koan, a word or phrase in Zen, the solving of which lies far beyond the intellect. Their "solving" leads in the end to satori, a flash of enlightenment by the light of which both heaven and earth shall pass away, and life be for the first time

[1] CHUANG TZU, Translation by GILES, p. 20.

utterly experienced. What is the answer? To reduce the Many to
the One is admirable, but still we are left gazing with rapturous
pride on our splendid handiwork, ourselves on the one hand, the
One on the other.

From the height of the "higher third" we viewed each opposite
from the viewpoint of both. There is, however, a fifth and final
stage. We must understand, by direct experience, that all is One,
then that the Many and the One are—what? Presumably
something above either. . . . No, this will not do. We are still in the
net of the opposites, still meshed in the net of intellectual juggling.
To understand this final solution of the opposites we must regress
for the moment, gain our second (intuitive) wind, and then rush
the enemies' defences straight up the hill.

In *The Essence of Buddhism,* Professor D. T. Suzuki, the
greatest living authority on Buddhist philosophy and the greatest
authority on Zen, has explained, so far as words, the symbols of
the intellect, can ever explain, the ultimate heights of Buddhist
reasoning. Only the philosophers of the Kegon School have dared
to advance beyond the Ring-pass-not of Indian thought. "Thou
art THAT," said the Brahman philosophers; "there is no more to be
said." But the Kegon School went further:

"The fundamental idea of Buddhism is to pass beyond the world of
opposites, a world built up by intellectual distinctions and
emotional defilements, and to realise a spiritual world of non-
distinction which involves achieving an absolute point of view. Yet
the Absolute is in no way distinct from the world of
discrimination, for to think so would be to place it opposite the
discriminating mind and so create a new duality."

Mutual identity, in brief, is not enough. "Thou art THAT" is far
from final, for there are still two things, though identical. How can
we understand that the two are at the same time One, yet several;
that just as the part exists by reason of the all, so it does not cease
to exist as a part by reason of its being the all? The intellect can toy
with the concept; only the intuition can understand.

"The one must be found in the two, with the two, and yet beyond
the two, that is to say, non-distinction is in distinction and
distinction is in non-distinction. . . . It is by this double process
only that the intellect can transcend itself."

But this state of a "perfect, mutual, unimpeded solution",—the

Kegon term is Jijimuge—though intellectually conceivable can only be intuitively experienced. It is the state of "Suchness", a term much used in Buddhist philosophy. In it both "thou" and "THAT" exist, as two and as one, and the cycle, or circle is complete. But to *know* this to be so, "to escape from the prison of rationality" as Dr. Suzuki calls the intellect, this is the way of Zen.

There is, however, a method of taking the problem in flank, as it were. It will be non-sense to the rational-minded, but such will read no further. Those who read on will expect increasing non-sense, for sense, the suburban villas of rational thought, will soon be left behind, and the mind will be free on the illimitable hills of its own inherent joy. Here, then, is the real solution to the problem of the opposites. Shall I tell it you? Consider a live goose in a bottle. How to get it out without hurting the goose or breaking the bottle? The answer is simple—"There, it's out!"[1]

Perhaps the point is already made by now that Zen is a matter of intuitive experience, and not intellectual understanding. But the fact is so fundamental to the Western thought-bound mind that I may be forgiven if I hammer it in.

Let us look at the position from the viewpoint of arrival, on the assumption, that is, that the goose is already out of the bottle. This interfused Oneness-Twoness *is*, and "the Essence of Mind is intrinsically pure". Bearing these two propositions in mind, whence comes the illusion of a separate duality? The answer is *manas,* that faculty of the lower mind which analyses, separates, divides, and thereby, in the illusion that its analysis is final, produces that ignorance which is the cause of suffering, including the root illusion of the reality of self. For self exists and yet is the not-self. It is the Self of which it is part and itself, and both, and neither. But it behaves as if it existed apart from the rest of itself. *Hinc illae lacrimae,* those tears which form the ocean of sorrow which all but drowns mankind. But the self views all things from its own level; it therefore regards all problems, tensions of the opposites, as real. The solution is simple. When a Brahman came to the Buddha, bearing a gift in either hand, the Buddha's greeting was the one word—"Drop it!" The Brahman dropped the gift in his right hand and advanced. "Drop it!" said the Blessed One, and the Brahman dropped the gift in his other hand. But as he advanced with empty hands, again the command rang out— "Drop it!" The Brahman was enlightened; his ignorance was

[1] This is the subject of the book's Wrapper and End-papers.

purged away. Yet, as I have learnt from bitter experience, it needs great courage to drop it, when "it" is the self, with all its beliefs, ideals, ambition and emotional ties.

There is another story which I have found delicious to apply. Two monks were returning to their monastery at nightfall, when they came to a ford. At the ford was a very pretty girl in despair at crossing the stream. Without pausing in his stride one of the monks picked her up, crossed the stream, put her down and walked on. The other monk was furious and dismayed. "How could you not only touch her but take her in your arms," he expostulated, remembering the Rules. And he continued to mutter the whole way home. Finally the first monk turned to him, as though with an effort dragging his thoughts to earth. "Oh, that girl. I left her at the ford. Are you still carrying her?" I sometimes think of the opposites as held apart with a fearful effort of the mind. How nice if one day I could let go, and listen to the "ping" with which they would spring back into unity!

Yet the intellect, for all its limitations, is essential, and must be developed to the full before it can be transcended. But it must not attempt a task too high for it.

"As long as intellect is confined to its proper sphere of work, all is well, but the moment it steps out of it and invades a field which does not belong to it, the outcome is disastrous. For this stepping out means the setting up of the self as a reality, and this is sure to collide with our ethical and religious valuation of human life; it also runs contrary to our spiritual insight into the nature of things."[1]

The intuition is the light which illumines the intellect. Unless there is an intellect the light will no more be seen than electric light is seen in the socket of a lamp which has no lamp. I do not apologise for repeating Roy Campbell's delicious lines *On some South African Novelists*:

> "*They praise the firm restraint with which you write.*
>   *I'm with you there of course.*
> *You use the snaffle and the curb all right,*
>   *But where's the bloody horse?*"

How often does one meet with those who wish to proceed beyond the intellect, and yet have not developed an intellect to transcend?

[1] *The Essence of Buddhism*, SUZUKI, p. II.

"If you can think—and not make thoughts your aim, If you can
meet with Triumph and Disaster and treat those two impostors
just the same," as Kipling advises in that poem of profound
philosophy, *If*—then you can use your thought-machinery, and
the emotions and the senses, and enjoy their user, for you will have
passed beyond their sway.

How shall we know when the intuition begins to awaken? The
process, like the development of any other function or power of
our complex nature, is, of course, gradual, but as it is the synthetic
faculty, the builder as distinct from the destroyer of the forms of
life, it will first appear as illumining the higher, abstract mind. All
rules of thought, all smooth manipulation of the concepts, as in
logic and dialectic, become increasingly tedious. All propositions
are alike seen to be one-sided and, as already shown, even the One
is a conception of limited value. Even the basic conventions of
thought become suspect, and are seen at last for what they are. A
famous Chinese painter was asked to paint for a friend a bamboo
forest. He painted it as usual with his brush and ink, but the ink
was red. The patron demurred. "Well," said the painter, "and in
what colour did you desire it?" "In black, of course," said the
patron. "And who," asked the artist, "ever saw a black-leaved
bamboo?"

Zen hates abstractions, and to the awakening intuition they
begin to pall. "Zen shuns abstractions, representations and figures
of speech. No real value is attached to such words as God, Buddha,
the soul, the Infinite, the One, and such-like words."[1] All words are
nets in which to ensnare the flow of life, and Zen regards them as a
necessary (and not always necessary) evil. Life moves on, and Zen
is life. A handful of the river is dead within the hand. Why hold it?
The Master's answers to the frequent question "What is Buddha?"
were therefore usually rude.

In the same way Zen refuses to slap labels. By this, my own quite
vulgar (and why not?) phrase, I mean the deplorable habit of
labelling all events, most things, and far too many people with an
epithet, or several. The weather is always "good" or "bad". It is
nothing of the kind. It is the weather. The same applies to the news,
one's neighbour's morals and the soup. An opinion is labelled
"right" or "wrong". It remains an opinion. Is it not sufficient to
take things as they are, knowing as we do that there is nothing

[1] *Introduction to Zen Buddhism*, p. 74.

either good or bad but thinking makes it so, and that what we seek is direct experience?

Paradox will assume new meaning, and be found to be the language which the intuition uses when the intellectual currency has failed. As R. H. Blyth points out, the use of paradox "does not spring from a desire to mystify the hearers or oneself. It arises from the inability of language to say two things at once." And again, "paradoxes are the bright banners of the liberty of the mind. ... Reason grips life with a strangle-hold, but life says, "To win is to lose," and as in Judo, "uses the power of the enemy to escape from it."[1]

The intuition releases the power of poetry, and the greatest poetry springs from it. The imagination, the heart of poetry, is progressively freed to create new channels of life, to awaken in the mind the springs of joy and laughter which the drear propriety of reasoning would banish from the world. If the intellect measures all worth with the yardstick of its own creation, the intuition takes no measurements at all. It knows that all life is one yet separate, and that all the forms of life have an equal validity. It moves, serene with certainty, and therefore tolerant of all that lives. Unlike cold reasoning it has no fear of laughter, and having risen above the ordered world in which the by-laws of logic decree without appeal what is "sense", it is free to indulge in non-sense, for it shines upon a plane where every two are discounted as another of the endless, tiresome but no longer limiting pairs of opposites.

To understand Zen, therefore, it is necessary to alter the prevailing attitude of mind. "When we try to talk about things beyond intellection we always make our start from intellection itself." Therefore, says Dr. Suzuki,

"when Zen-experiences are talked about they sound empty as if they had no positive value. But Zen proposes that we effect a complete *volte-face* and take our stand first upon Zen-experience itself and then observe things—the world of being and non-being—from the point of view of the experience."

The results are profound.

"We are no longer a plaything of *karma*, of 'cause and effect', of

---

[1] *Zen in English Literature*, pp. 180, 193.

birth and death; values of the changing world are no longer permanent ones. ..."[1]

Henceforth the mind moves on unceasingly, dropping all things, even the fetter of thought. It moves, refusing to sit down in the noblest concept, and seeking nothing lest the search be a fetter to limit its constant flow. "Do not strive to seek after the true," writes a Zen Master, "only cease to cherish opinions."[2] The result is an increasingly subjective attitude of mind, an active-passive acceptance of circumstance, which allows things to happen, in the mind within and in the larger part of the mind we perceive outside of us. Asked, "What is Tao?", the Master Nansen replied, "Usual life is very Tao." "And how does one accord with it?" asked the enquirer. "If you try to accord with it you will get away from it," was the reply. "If any man be unhappy," said the Greek slave, Epictetus, "let him know that it is by reason of himself alone."

Or, as Count Keyserling said, somewhat later,

"One ought to get so far as to become entirely independent of the accident of one's external surroundings, that is to say, one ought to have such complete mastery over one's inner surroundings that, by changing it at will, as the chameleon changes his colour, one would attain what is otherwise only more or less attainable by the shrewd consideration of external influences."[3]

All of which the Patriarch Wei Lang expressed more pithily by saying

"Our mind should stand aloof from cirumstances, and on no account should we allow them to influence the function of our mind."[4]

So much for a rapid survey of an enormous subject. It is enough to add that Zen is first and last a matter of experience. Hence the suggestion that he who fears the experience, or still believes that the counters of conceptual thought will serve as substitutes, should abandon now this humble attempt to feed the awakening faculty of immediate knowledge with the truth of Zen. Words have their uses, but the noblest words are but noises in the air. They die, and in the end is silence, silence and a finger pointing the Way.

[1] *Philosophy, East and West*, p. 119.
[2] Quoted in *The Perennial Philosophy*, ALDOUS HUXLEY, p. 153.
[3] *Travel Diary of a Philosopher*, II, 132.
[4] *The Sutra of Wei Lang*, p. 49.

Chapter 2

The Birth of Zen Buddhism

It is said—and what is tradition but truth in the robes of poetry?—that once, when the Buddha was seated with his Bhikkhus on the Mount of Holy Vulture, a Brahma-Raja came to him and, offering him a golden flower, asked him to preach the Dharma. The Blessed One received the flower and, holding it aloft, gazed at it in perfect silence. After a while the Venerable Mahâkaśyapa smiled. Such, it is said, is the origin of Zen Buddhism. But as Dr. Suzuki points out:

"This smile is not an ordinary one such as we often exchange on the plane of distinction; it came out of the deepest recesses of his nature, where he and Buddha and all the rest of the audience move and have their being. No words are needed when this is reached. A direct insight across the abyss of human understanding is indicated."[1]

It is further said that the Wisdom which this smile revealed was handed down through the centuries by twenty-eight successive Patriarchs, the Buddha himself being the first, and the last the Indian philosopher Bodhidharma, who arrived in China in the middle of the sixth century A.D. and became the founder of the Zen School of Buddhism. Many of the intervening Patriarchs were mighty men in the world of Indian thought, and Aśvagosha, Nâgârjuna and Vasubandhu, to name but three, will be honoured as long as Indian wisdom is preserved.

The recorded history of Zen Buddhism is less romantic. Its origin, of course, is the Buddha's Enlightenment, for as the whole of Zen Buddhism exists as a vehicle for this direct Enlightenment, there would without it be no Zen Buddhism and, in this present world of *avidyâ*, ignorance, no Zen.

This all but unutterable Wisdom, the fruits of his spiritual

[1] *Essence of Buddhism*, p. 22.

experience, the Blessed One taught to his chosen few disciples. Such as they understood they remembered; such as they remembered they handed down. In this state, two hundred years or more after the Passing, the Pali Canon began to be written down. But already the Sangha, the Monastic followers of the All-Enlightened One, were splitting into manifold sects, the grounds of cleavage being partly doctrinal and partly monastic discipline. Famous pundits are still debating the genesis of these various sects, and the dates at which and the reasons for which the Mahayana or Great Vehicle, as it called itself, began to diverge from the Hinayana, the Small Vehicle as it called the older School, or the Thera Vâda, the Teaching of the Elders, as the latter called itself. To students of Zen, however, these niceties of historical research are of little importance, and of none to the man who has once, for a thousandth part of a second, known *satori*. For the blaze of light which floods the mind from its own eternal inwardness when thoughts of "this" and "that" are for the moment purged away illumines unforgettably one tiny corner of the Real, and history and all that is bound in time has little interest more. It is enough, therefore, that in the course of time the fertile Indian mind began to work on the basic principles of the Ancient Wisdom which the Buddha had once more presented to mankind. The Teaching spread, south to Ceylon, south-east to Burma, Siam, Cambodia, east into China, and thence to Korea and Japan, north into the locked and silent plateau of Tibet.

It seems to have reached China in the first century A.D. In what form it came is by no means clear, but the earliest Buddhist Scriptures to be translated into Chinese were a collection of sayings culled from a number of Sutras, or Discourses, the collection being known as *The Sutra of 42 Sections*, which may be described as a Hinayana work modified to express the views of Mahayana adherents. This was not Zen. It was, however, a prelude to its birth, for it was the Chinese genius working on the raw material of Indian thought which, with contributions from Confucian and Taoist sources, produced, with Bodhidharma as midwife, the essentially Chinese School of Ch'an or, as the Japanese later called it, Zen Buddhism.

Suffice it to say that the two main schools of Buddhism are as the two sides of a coin. All that is relatively stressed in one is discoverable in the other in a less developed form; and the two are one in the sense that men and women are one, two sides of a human being. The Thera Vâda, now to be found in Ceylon, Burma, Siam and Cambodia, is certainly the older School. It is more orthodox; clings harder to the wording of its Pali Canon, emphasises moral philosophy and the prime importance of the individual's working out his own salvation before he attempts to "save" his neighbour or the world. If it is puritan in its cold insistence on character-building, it is yet suffused with the sweetness of a reasonable, unemotional pursuit of a Way which leads—did not the Blessed One prove it abundantly?—to the heart's desire, that peace which comes when the heart is empty of desire, and self is dead.

The Mahayana adopted all of this, but added upon these broad and, some say, all-sufficient premises a vast erection of emotion-thought which flowered in time in the intuitive white light of Zen. The Indian mind was never satisfied with the teachings, moral and philosophical, of Thera Vâda Buddhism; and soon the precepts of right living were developed into principles of cosmic truth. The Buddha, from a man who attained Enlightenment, came to be viewed as the Principle of Enlightenment which dwells in all. As such his forms were multiplied, and fast on the heels of iconography came ritual; a moral philosophy became a religion. The metaphysical heights of Indian thought were climbed, equalled, and finally surpassed. The Bodhisattva, he who dedicates his life and the fruits of life to his fellow men, replaced the Arhat, he who strives for his own perfection before he presumes to lead his brother on the Way. Compassion was raised to equality with Wisdom; the depth of the Thera Vâda was turned to an expansion of interest which embraced all living things.

These changes are, so it seems to me, as inevitable as they are right if a system of thought is to claim, as Buddhism claims, to be all-embracing, and to supply all human spiritual needs. In the vast field of present Buddhism there is to be found religion, philosophy, metaphysics, mysticism, psychology, and much of the science which is claimed as a western discovery of the last few years. There is also room for the poetry, the love of nature and beauty and the sense of fun which is native to the Chinese character; and behind it all is a vast tradition of spiritual truth only part of which is ever recorded and little of which has ever appeared in a western tongue. In a general way, and one must generalise in the broadest terms, the Schools are as complementary as the night and day. The austerity of the Southern School is offset by the religious fervour of some of the northern sects, and the intensive-

expansive, practical-mystical, developing-preserving tendencies
of the respective points of view are neither good nor bad, pure nor
impure Buddhism, but parts of an inseverable whole. If in the
exuberance of spiritual thought some later teachers of the
Mahayana developed methods and technique which seem to run
counter to the Teaching of the Buddha as early recorded in the Pali
Canon, the tolerant Buddhist mind would at least admit that
extremist doctrines, such as those of the Pure Land School, may
possibly be true, while reserving the right to hold, as I do hold, that
it is difficult to see how they can fairly be labelled Buddhism. Yet
the common ground of most of the Schools of Buddhism, North or
South, is far, far larger than all their differences, and beyond all
complementary emphasis on this or that particular doctrine is the
direct, supreme, and to us ineffable Experience of the All-
Enlightened One.

When Bodhidharma (Tamo to the Japanese) arrived in China,
the Mahayana was still only partly developed, but the initial
hostility to Buddhism, so notable on its first arrival, seems to have
died down. The Chinese are a practical people and disliked both
the celibacy and the begging habits of the Buddhist monks. A man
should work for his living, they said, and part of his duty is to
provide for the memory of his father and to raise up sons to care
for his own. Moreover, they deeply distrusted the metaphysics of
Indian thought as displayed in the Sutras already translated, and
although some of these Sutras, later found to be closely akin to
Zen, such as the *Vimalakirti*, had already been translated by the
famous Indian Buddhist, Kumarajiva, the Chinese needed a
transference of Indian thought itself into the Chinese idiom before
Buddhism could be assimilated into their national life. In the
result, it was left to the individual Chinese thinker to choose from
the wealth of material such Sutras as seemed to him of value; and
about such thinkers and their Commentaries upon some favoured
Sutra sprang up the manifold schools or sects which together in
time amounted to Chinese Buddhism. Thus, for example, were the
Tendai and the Kegon Schools developed respectively from the
Mâdhyamika and Yogâchârya Schools of Indian Buddhism, and thus
about the *Avatamsaka Sutra*, introduced to the Chinese mind in
the fifth century by Buddhabhadra, was built up the School which
later developed into Zen.

But the Chinese mind, essentially rationalist and humanist,
though with its mystical feeling developed in Taoism, produced an

immense change in the form of Buddha Dharma. From the luminous heights of Indian thought was developed an emphasis on inner values which at the same time had to express itself and be expressed in action and hard work. Wisdom to the Chinese thinker is never an escape from worldly life. As shown in the famous Cowherding pictures, when the pilgrim has so controlled his lower self that he has reached the final goal, he does not linger there.

> "To return to the Origin, to be back at the Source—already a
>   false step this!
> Far better it is to stay at home; ...
> ... he comes out into the market-place;
> Daubed with mud and ashes, how broadly he smiles!
> There is no need for the miraculous power of the gods
> For he touches, and lo! the dead trees come into full bloom."[1]

Hence the exciting statement in that famous Chinese classic, *The Secret of the Golden Flower*.

"The holy science takes as a beginning the knowledge of where to stop, and as an end, stopping at the highest good. Its beginning is beyond polarity and it empties again beyond polarity."[2]

The concentration upon inner values and processes was soon to pervade all Schools of the Mahayana. As the sixth Chinese Patriarch of Zen in the seventh century taught,

"Our mind should stand aloof from circumstances and on no account should we allow them to influence the function of our mind."

And again, as illustrating this absolute idealism:

"You should know that so far as Buddha-nature is concerned, there is no difference between an enlightened man and an ignorant one. What makes the difference is that one realises it, while the other is ignorant of it."

A better illustration still, perhaps, is the famous story of the flag.

"It happened one day, when a pennant was blown about by the wind, two Bhikkhus entered into dispute as to what it was that was in motion, the wind or the pennant. As they could not settle their

---

[1] *Essays in Zen Buddhism*, I, 365–66.
[2] P. 66.

difference I submitted to them that it was neither, and that actually what moved was their own mind."[1]

It was easy, therefore, for the Chinese mind to adopt with enthusiasm the first verse of the *Dhammapada,* perhaps the most popular Scripture of all the Pali Canon. "All that we are is the result of what we have thought, it is made by our thoughts. ..." Man is indeed the product of his own past thought and actions, and it follows that his thoughts and actions today decide his condition tomorrow, and in the larger tomorrows of his later lives on earth.

The Chinese are concerned with processes, rather than with results. Things have their value, but all things are in a state of flux. Contentment of mind, therefore, is to be found in the flow of life itself, not in the buildings, either of hands or thoughts, which house that life for the space of a butterfly day or the brief span of the clay's mortality. Zen, therefore, with its insistence on direct experience, unmindful of the forms of wisdom from which the life too swiftly ebbs away, was extremely acceptable to the Chinese mind, and if this suitability has been emphasised it is because the Chinese are in a way the British of the East, and most of the attributes above described might as well be applied to the average Englishman.

This Mahayana development was, of course, of gradual growth, and it was in the midst of the process that Bodhidharma, "the bearded barbarian", arrived from India, and into the cross-currents of the stream of Chinese thought threw the depth-charge of Zen. His four propositions which, even if the formula was produced later, summarised his purpose and technique, were as follows:

> "*A special transmission outside the Scriptures;*
> *No dependence upon words and letters;*
> *Direct pointing to the soul of man;*
> *Seeing into one's own nature."*

In brief, a direct transmission of the Wisdom without depending on words, and the direct seeing into one's own nature.

At a time when some of the best brains of the country were translating and writing commentaries on the metaphysical scriptures of Indian Buddhism, this brutal frontal attack on the

---

[1] *Sutra of Wei Lang,* pp. 49, 27 and 24.

citadel of truth must have caused an enormous sensation. Hence Dr. Suzuki's phrase that Zen was the Chinese revolt against Buddhism. Yet it was not until the time of Hui-neng, a hundred and fifty years later, that Zen became a genuinely Chinese form of Buddhism, to have immense effect on the Chinese art of the T'ang Dynasty. It is to be observed, however, that none of this apparent extension of the original teachings was regarded as moving away from them. Bodhidharma claimed to be returning to the spirit of the Buddha's teaching, and if—and this is the very foundation stone of Zen—Buddhism is a record of Buddha's Enlightenment, he was right. It was those who petrified the flow of truth in the written word of the Scriptures who were slaying the Dharma, and Zen, from this point of view, was the dredging of a stream made foul with ritual and worship, with the niceties of logic and rational philosophy, and the débris of all manner of conceptual thought.

Our knowledge of Bodhidharma is largely derived from *The Records of the Transmission of the Lamp*, a book which, though written in A.D. 1004, is based on contemporary records now destroyed. Our second authority is *Biographies of the High Priests* by Tao-hsuan, compiled in A.D. 645. The records differ in detail, but the outline is clear. Bodhidharma will live for ever in the annals of Zen Buddhism for introducing into it the element of *satori*, the im-mediate experience of truth as distinct from understanding about it. Nor did he merely offer this original contribution to Chinese Buddhism; he lived it. He was born in south India—tradition says in Big Conjeeveram—and studied Buddhism under his teacher, Prajnatara, for forty years. From Prajnatara he acquired by merit the patriarchate of the Dhyâna or Zen School, thus becoming the 28th Indian, as he was to become the 1st Chinese, Patriarch. On the death of his Teacher he sailed for China, arriving in A.D. 520. The Emperor Wu at once invited him to his capital, the modern Nanking. On his arrival the Emperor, a most devout Buddhist, began to boast of his good works. "I have built many temples and monasteries," he said. "I have copied the sacred books of the Buddha. I have converted Bhikkhus and Bhikkhunis. Now what is my merit?" To which this silent, ferocious-looking Indian Buddhist replied, "None whatever, your Majesty!"

The Emperor, taken aback at this brutal answer, tried again. "What is to be considered as the First Principle of the Dharma?" he asked. "Vast Emptiness, and nothing holy therein," replied the Patriarch. "Who, then," asked the Emperor, not unreasonably, "now confronts me?" "I have no idea," said Bodhidharma. Thus, in a brief but historic interview, was laid the foundation of a School which became the dominant sect of China, and is one of the two main schools of Japanese Buddhism, having enormously influenced both countries in their character, culture, art and philosophy.

Bodhidharma, having introduced in his own inimitable style the teaching and technique of Zen, retired to the country, and in the Shao Lin monastery meditated in silence for nine years. Finally there came to him a former Confucian scholar, by name Shen Kuang, who asked to be instructed in the Dharma. The Master took no notice. For seven days and nights the petitioner waited in the snow and finally, to prove to the obdurate teacher the life-and-death sincerity of his demand, he cut off his arm, and sent it in. The Master saw him. "Pray," said the exhausted student, "pacify my mind." "Let me see your mind," said the Master, "and I will pacify it." "I cannot produce this mind which troubles me so much," said the would-be pupil. "Then I have pacified your mind," said Bodhidharma, and the pupil was at last enlightened.

The truth of the story is immaterial, but as a most dramatic account of the birth in China of Zen principles it is of highest value. And that is nearly all that we know of the founder of Zen Buddhism, whose fierce, aggressive, bearded head has been the theme of a thousand artists from that day to this. Even his end is a matter of mystery, but it is in the true tradition of Zen to believe that he was last seen at a tremendous age returning through the Western Gates of China with one of his sandals on his head. This may be comic; it may have been symbolic; from such a man it was most certainly Zen.

The Confucian monk whose soul had been so swiftly pacified became the 2nd Chinese Patriarch under the name of Hui-ke. To him the Master handed the *Lankâvatâra Sutra* as containing an epitome of the secret of Zen; hence the popularity of this Sutra with students of Zen today. It would seem that he was the first Zen martyr, for he was put to death in A.D. 593 for teaching a false doctrine. He spent his life in preaching Zen to the lowest strata of society, and the popularity of this beggar in rags aroused opposition from the forces of well-fed orthodoxy. Before he died, however, he passed on the robe which had come to be the insignia of the Patriarchate to Seng-ts'an, who survives in history as the author of the Hsin Hsin Ming, a metrical rendering of the principles of Zen. A translation of the poem appears in Dr. Suzuki's *Essays in Zen Buddhism* (I, 182-87). Here in print is the way to dissolve the Opposites.

The fourth Patriarch was Tao-hsin. He had asked the previous Master, "Pray show me the way to deliverance." Said the Master, "Who has put you under restraint?" When the enquirer answered, "No one," the Master enquired in turn, "Then why do you seek deliverance?"

Under Tao-hsin (580-651) Zen Buddhism was divided into two. One part did not survive the passing of its founder. The other branch was headed by Hung-jen, later the fifth Patriarch, who lives today in the famous *Sutra of Wei Lang* (Hui-neng), the sixth Patriarch.

Like a famous character in a later religion than Buddhism, Hung-jen prepared the way for another greater than himself. This was Hui-neng, whose name, according to a southern dialect, may be pronounced Wei-lang and is better known in the West as such by reason of the late Mr. Wong Mou-lam's translation of his famous "Platform-Sutra". Under the fifth Patriarch, Hung-jen, Zen rose from a small retiring sect of earnest students to a position where it was ready to support a full proclamation of Zen. This was Hui-neng's destiny, and he became the second founder of Zen Buddhism, the mind responsible for developing Zen into a purely Chinese form of Buddhism, both in its teaching and means of expression. He was poorly educated, and was never a scholar in the usual sense of the word. His story is told in his own Sutra, which ranks as one of the classics of eastern literature. In it the close affinities with Taoism are clearly shown, and indeed the words Tao and Dharma are at times with some of the later Masters used synonymously. No student of Zen can fail to study this diamond mine of Zen, or indeed the Commentary upon it which Dr. Suzuki has written under the title of *The Zen Doctrine of No-Mind*. Here it is sufficient to point out that the failure of Hui-neng's rival, Shen-hsiu, to receive the robe from the fifth Patriarch caused him to secede from the latter's following, and to set up a northern school of his own. This Shen-hsiu was an ex-Confucian and, with his school of "gradual" enlightenment, was given Imperial protection and encouragement, but within a hundred years of the founder's death it had utterly disappeared. The "Sudden" School of Hui-neng prospered mightily. As Dr. Suzuki says,

"The latent energy that had been stored up during the time of naturalisation suddenly broke out in active work, and Zen had almost a triumphal march through the whole land of Cathay."

Soon after the passing of Hui-neng, who appointed no successor, the Master Hyakujo founded the system, still in use, of the Meditation Hall. In all other schools of Buddhism, and in most other religions, an image of the Founder is the central feature of a temple or a monastery. Only in Zen is the Meditation Hall of paramount importance, and when by the tenth century the *koan* (for an explanation of which please wait for the chapter on Zen Technique) had come to be the recognised means of "device" for attaining *satori*, Enlightenment, all the main features of Zen Buddhism were in being, and have hardly varied in the thousand years which separate that period from today. It was in Japan, however, that the tradition was best carried on, for by the thirteenth century Zen Buddhism in China had begun to lose its initial impulse. As early as the seventh century Zen had reached Japan, but it was not until the twelfth century that a Tendai monk called Eisai crossed into China to study Zen, and returned to found a Zen monastery in Kyoto. But Kyoto was the headquarters of Shingon and Tendai Buddhism, and it was in Kamakura, under the powerful wing of the Hojo family, that Zen took root in Japan. Eisai founded the Japanese branch of Rinzai Zen. Soto Zen arrived a few years later, in the hands of his pupil, Dogen, while the third of the three sects of Zen, the Obaku, was introduced by Ingen in the seventeenth century, and is now but a part of Rinzai Zen. The difference between the schools is chiefly the importance given to the *koan* exercises. In the Rinzai sect this is still the basis of spiritual development; in the Soto sect it is far less used. Zen was seized by the military class and made its own. The Tendai and Kegon sects of Buddhism, both in a way synthetic philosophies made up from diverse material, were too philosophic for the Japanese knights of the Middle Ages, who were yet most cultured men. Jodo, on the other hand, and its later extremist derivative, the Pure Land School of Shin, needing no learning, and demanding but a constant invocation to the spirit of Buddhahood, were more acceptable to the people. Shingon Buddhism, with its emphasis on ritual, was extremely popular at Court. Zen was a warrior creed. It called for action, for the most rigorous self-discipline, for self-reliance, for contempt of death. So did the iron cult of Bushido, the Way of the Knightly Virtue. The warrior owned but his swords, and his swords were his honour and his life. By the larger he lived: by the smaller he would, at his Lord's behest or when his honour was injured, die by his own hand. This was a man's life, and it needed a man's religion. Zen is "poor", for the heart must be emptied of all else if the light is to enter. It calls for that loneliness of heart which woos the Absolute, for adaptability to outward circumstance, for contempt of the accidents of changing form, and yet, being, as Dr. Suzuki calls it, radical empiricism, it is utterly practical and "lives in facts" to the utter exclusion of ideas. Nought must come between a man and his loyalty to his Lord; nought must intervene between a man and the mind's experience. To think, when the enemy's sword is descending, is death; to act, and to act rightly as the result of years of training, here is life, and the flow of life, with no intermediate.

At a later stage we shall see how this virile, stern yet laughing philosophy of life produced in Japan great art, great warriors and a culture second to none. Cradled by a warrior class, it is not surprising that Zen in Japan is violent in the means employed. But are we not all warriors? As the Buddha is given as saying in the Canon of the Southern School,

"We wage war, O Bhikkhus; therefore are we called warriors.... For lofty virtue, for high endeavour, for sublime wisdom, for those do we wage war. Therefore are we called warriors."

We must take the Kingdom of Heaven by storm; only then shall we find that we have never left it.

Buddhism recognises no authority for a spiritual truth; hence its tolerance. But the transmission of the doctrine is regarded as of great importance. Each Zen Master must be sanctioned by his Master, and he who teaches without such sanction is regarded as heterodox. Thus, through all the changes of Japanese national life, from the feudal system which extended into the nineteenth century to a modernism based on American patterns, still the tradition is kept high, and if the means of arousing understanding are today less violent, the Roshi or Zen Master is a man of tremendous spiritual development, and claims to be in the direct line of the Buddha's direct experience. The power of the light within must vary with the individual; the lighting of the lamp is the purpose of Zen Buddhism, and the light is Zen.

If only for the sake of tidiness, I must finish this chapter with a brief description of the coming of Zen to Europe.

In 1906 the Open Court Publishing Company of Chicago published *Sermons of a Buddhist Abbot* by Soyen Shaku, then the Lord-Abbot of Engakuji at Kamakura, the monastery where Dr. Suzuki, his pupil, is living and writing today. These reported sermons, together with a translation by Dr. Suzuki of the *Sutra of 42 Sections,* were the first information for the West on the subject of Zen. In the following year Dr. Suzuki wrote a paper for the *Journal of the Pali Text Society* of London which, so far as I know, was the first presentation to England of the meaning as distinct from the mere existence of Zen Buddhism. In 1913, Luzac and Co. of London published *The Religion of the Samurai* by Kaiten Nukariya, an admirable textbook about Zen, though purely on the plane of the intellect. E. J. Harrison's *The Fighting Spirit of Japan*, published in London in the same year, has a chapter on Zen, but the subject is treated without understanding.

In 1921 Dr. Suzuki founded and edited *The Eastern Buddhist,* for which he wrote between that date and its final issue in 1939 a great many articles on Zen, many of which were used as the basis for his later books. The circulation in England, however, was never large, and the same presumably applied to a thirty-page booklet written by Arthur Waley in 1922 on *Zen Buddhism and its Relation to Art*. To all intents and purposes, therefore, the general public had only *The Religion of the Samurai* for their study of Zen until Dr. Suzuki began, in 1927, the publication of his long series of works which the Buddhist Society, London, are now in the process of republishing in England.

The first volume of *Essays in Zen Buddhism* opened a new world of vision for the many thousands who read it, and the following two volumes, and the later works as listed in the Bibliography at the end of this volume, have now made Zen available, to the extent that it can ever be conveyed in print, to the English-speaking world. It is right to add that Dr. J. B. Pratt, who in 1928 produced his monumental work *The Pilgrimage of Buddhism*, seems to have acquired his knowledge of Zen without reference to these Essays of Dr. Suzuki's, though as he adds the latter's name to those who had helped him, it is probable that he had read the volumes of *The Eastern Buddhist* from which the Essays were more or less compiled. By 1932 the three main Sutras used in Zen were available in English. William Gemmell had translated *The Diamond Sutra* in 1912. *The Sutra of Wei Lang* reached England in 1930, and Dr. Suzuki's *Studies in the Lankâvatâra Sutra* and the translated text, *The Lankâvatâra Sutra,* appeared in 1930 and 1932 respectively. To these must be added the *Huang Po Doctrine of Universal Mind* (trans. Chu Ch'an) and other Zen Sutras now being published by the Buddhist Society in London as fast as members in China can send them in competent translation.

From 1930 onwards books and articles on Zen began to increase in quantity, yet all of them were influenced by, if not entirely based upon, the works of Dr. Suzuki. A section in my *What is Buddhism?* (1928), Mrs. Adams Beck's very lovely work. *The Garden of Vision* (1929), Dwight Goddard's *The Buddha's Golden Path* (1930), these and the steady output of Dr. Suzuki made Zen increasingly known. Then came the war, but after it, when I found the Professor, hale and hearty at seventy-six, in his house in Engakuji at Kamakura, he told me of eighteen further volumes on Buddhism which he had written during the war, and which were waiting to be translated into English as soon as he or some other competent translator could find the time. Some of these will be published in England in the next few years; his famous "Address to the Emperor of Japan" has already passed into a second edition under the title of *The Essence of Buddhism.*

And now new writers are beginning to appear. Mr. R. H. Blyth, who is writing the Professor's life, has himself after sixteen years in a Korean Zen monastery written, as a teacher of English in Japan, a rich compendious work, *Zen in English Literature and Oriental Classics.* The Buddhist Society, London, are publishing the collected works, slim though as yet they are, of W. J. Gabb, the author of *Beyond the Intellect,* and *Tales of Tokuzan.*[1] I have written a little of Zen in my *Studies in the Middle Way,* and a brief exordium which I have called *Walk On!* Material for study is, therefore, available now in western lands, for books have appeared in German, notably *Zen, der lebendige Buddhismus in Japan,* by Ohasama and Faust, and Dr. Suzuki's *Essays* have appeared in French.[2] Yet words are but marks on paper, or noises in the air; in the end it is work, hard work in the practice of direct, im-mediate living which alone produces the direct, im-mediate experience of Zen.

[1] Now reprinted, with new matter, as *The Goose is Out* (1956).
[2] See Bibliography, p. 163, which incorporates later titles in English. In French the latest work is H. Benoit. *La Doctrine Supreme,* later published in English as *The Supreme Doctrine.*

Chapter 3

The Nature of Zen Buddhism

There are men, and plenty of them, who think that when something has been classified in accordance with the prevailing system of filing, they know more about it. But nothing has happened; such men know nothing more about a flower to which they have in triumph added a Latin name of fourteen syllables, and they are no nearer to the spiritual experience known as Zen by announcing that Zen is this or that. Zen is, and the noises made in its presence affect it no more than a flower is impressed by its labelling.

Yet questions are asked, and some of the questions are worth answering.

Is Zen Buddhism a religion? It depends, of course, upon what is meant by religion. "It is not a religion in the sense that the term is popularly understood; for Zen has no God to worship, no ceremonial rites to observe, no future abode to which the dead are destined, and, last of all, Zen has no soul whose welfare is to be looked after by somebody else and whose immortality is a matter of intense concern with some people. Zen is free from all these dogmatic and 'religious' encumbrances."[1] If, on the other hand, it is as Professor Whitehead conceives it, the answer is otherwise. "It is the vision of something which stands beyond, behind and within the passing flux of immediate things; something which is a remote possibility and yet the greatest of present facts; something that gives meaning to all that passes and yet eludes apprehension; something whose possession is the final good, and yet is beyond all reach; something which is the ultimate ideal, and the hopeless quest."[2]

Much depends on the alleged relationship of the Teacher to the Teaching which is later taught in his name. No Teacher ever

---

[1] *Introduction to Zen Buddhism*, p. 14.
[2] Quoted in *Diagnosis of Man*, WALKER, p. 100.

founds a religion. He teaches, and men listen to his Teaching. He passes, as all else passes, and about the memory of his Teaching men build up, as a wall about some holy object, a system of thought and doctrine, of ceremonial and worship, which all too soon bears little resemblance to the Teacher's own attempt to promulgate his spiritual experience. In time, indeed, the religion becomes a substitute for the actual experience, and as such becomes evil. As Dr. Jung points out, "Creeds are codified and dogmatised forms of original religious experience," and these are easily used as shields against the terrors of direct experience. "What is usually and generally called 'religion' is to such an amazing degree a substitute that I ask myself seriously whether this kind of 'religion', which I prefer to call a creed, has not an important function in human society. The substitution has the obvious purpose of replacing immediate experience by a choice of suitable symbols invested in a solidly organised dogma and ritual."[1] And as the purpose of Zen is "direct seeing into the heart of man", anything which stands between a man and such direct experience is evil, to be thrust aside as a barrier which intervenes between the seeker and his goal.

Yet religion can be used as a raft whereby to cross the raging flood of Samsara, and to reach the farther shore. But he is a fool who carries the raft thereafter, and religion is at the best a means to an end, to be cast aside when its purpose is fulfilled. And without doubt religions may be used to heal: "All religions," says Dr. Jung, "are therapies for the sorrows and disorders of the soul," for when the part is sick it seeks reunion with the whole, and religion, a re-binding, is a means for effecting, by penance and sacrifice and inward prayer, a re-integration of the soul. And in a way, it would seem, we are all sick men, for only in a state of consciousness beyond the desires of self lies health or wholeness, and until we find that light within we sit in the darkness of the soul's disease.

It seems that man must have a religion, even though it should bear a disguise remote from its normal seeming. "Having lost the old faith, they turn eagerly to new ones, and science, psycho-analysis, spiritualism, social reform and nationalism have all in turn acted as substitutes for religion."[2] Of these the most evil is the State. God, a convenient invention, may at least be a God of love. The State is cold, impersonal, has neither warmth nor love nor

[1] *Psychology and Religion*, pp. 6 and 52.
[2] *Diagnosis of Man*, WALKER, p. 243.

mystery: is purely conscious, having no controllable relation with the vast forces of the unconscious mind, and being without heart, it rejects the devotee in the moment of his greatest need. Like all things large, it has no meaning, and I for one hate all things large, be it a department store, a limited company or a world society. These lack humanity; they make and are bound by foolish rules; they do not care. But "the race is run by one and one and never by two and two" and only one man, not a crowd, or a nation or a committee finds deliverance. In the end the Truth is beyond all formulation. Is it not written in the *Diamond Sutra*, "Subhuti, what do you think? Has the Tathagata attained the Consummation of Incomparable Enlightenment? Has the Tathagata a teaching to enunciate?" And Subhuti answered, "As I understand the Buddha's meaning there is no formulation of truth called Consummation of Incomparable Enlightenment. Moreover, the Tathagata has no formulated teaching to enunciate. Wherefore? Because the Tathagata has said that truth is uncontainable and inexpressible. It either is or it is not. Thus it is that this unformulated Principle is the foundation of the different systems of all the sages."[1] In brief, although Zen Buddhism is in some sense a religion, Zen itself is the light of all religions; it is not one of them.

Is Zen Buddhism truly a part of Buddhism? Or is it accidental that this fierce, direct approach to reality flowered from the stem of Buddhism, when it might equally have flowered elsewhere? To the extent that "Buddhism" limits Zen, Zen is not Buddhism, for "anything that has the semblance of an external authority is rejected by Zen".[2] On the other hand, as Dr. Suzuki says elsewhere, "If Buddhism were to develop in the Far East so as to satisfy the spiritual cravings of its people, it had to grow into Zen"[3], which accords with his constant statement that Zen was the Chinese way of absorbing and applying Buddhism. Dr. Ananda Coomaraswamy begins by describing Zen Buddhism as the more philosophical and mystical aspect of the Mahayana, and as essentially indifferent to iconolatry and to scriptural authority. "This phase of Mahayana is little determined by special forms, and can scarcely be said to have any other creed than that the kingdom of heaven is in the heart of man. This school of thought," he concludes "most fully represents the Mahayana as a world

[1] *The Jewel of Transcendental Wisdom.* Trans. PRICE, p. 32.
[2] *Introduction to Zen Buddhism*, p. 21.
[3] *Ibid*, p. 9.

religion".[1] This is on account of its amazing flexibility. Being bound to no forms, using any or no philosophy and all convenient manner of technique, Zen is the flowering of the mind from the seeds of spiritual experience. It is based upon, draws its life from and actually is the Enlightenment which made Prince Siddhartha, Kumar of the Kshatriyas, the Buddha, the Enlightened One. Zen is therefore the *Buddh* in Buddhism, and "the definition of Buddhism must be that of the life-force which carries forward a spiritual movement called Buddhism". One may therefore agree with Professor Kaiten Nukariya, "Beyond all doubt Zen belongs to Mahayanism yet this does not imply that it depends on the scriptural authority of that school, because it does not trouble itself about the Canon, whether it be Hinayana or Mahayana, or whether it was directly spoken by Shakya Muni or written by some later Buddhists." Or, one might add, written by a small boy on the nursery wall or published in the local railway guide. If it appeals to the intuition it is food for Zen; if not, it has no more value than a speech on politics. Zen Buddhism, in brief, appears in and uses the vehicle built for it called Zen Buddhism; it also appears on the race-course, in the cathedral, and in the W.C.

Within the fold of the Mahayana, Zen Buddhism is often referred to as the Meditation School. It uses meditation, and, as already explained, the Zen-Do or Meditation Hall in a Zen monastery is the very heart of the community, but its meditation is far from the meaning of that term in India. There is no deliberate abstraction from the things of sense. Non-attachment, the cure for desire which is the cause of suffering, is an incidental development. Nor does it analyse phenomena, as in the Southern School of Buddhism, with a view to understanding their essential evanescence, and "soul-lessness". Rather it seeks to develop the intuition, which cares not for the opposites and is neither attracted nor repelled. It is the Meditation Sect in that it uses profound meditation, with or without the *koan* exercise, as a means to the awakening of Buddhi, the intuitive faculty which is the light of Enlightenment. But it is by no means the Contemplative Sect which certain armchair scholars seem to believe. No one who has lived in a Zen monastery would describe the life of the monks as contemplative in the sense applied to certain Christian Orders. "No work, no food," was laid down as the rule for the monks one thousand years ago, and the general impression of the daily round

[1] *Buddha and the Gospel of Buddhism*, p. 253.

is one of strenuous activity. A *koan* may as well be solved with a
spade in the hand as in locked, ecstatic silence, and the humblest
chores are carried out with the same efficiency and good-will as the
longest session of deep meditation in the Zen-Do.

What, then, is the place of Zen Buddhism in the field of the
Mahayana? It is a revolt from the formalism inherent in the
Japanese character. Outwardly, there are services for the people,
with the officiating priests appearing in the most gorgeous robes.
Inwardly there is only the silent striving for direct experience, and
every "form", however tenuous, is looked upon as a net to ensnare
the awakening consciousness. Like a butterfly it rests on the
branch of the tree of Wisdom which men for the moment call
Buddhism. If it fluttered away it would still be—what it is.

Is Zen but a form of pantheism? Yes and no. If pantheism
means, as my dictionary suggests, that the whole universe is God,
or that every part of the universe is a manifestation of God, then
Zen is not pantheism, for Zen would deny the validity of the partial
conception of God. The Zen view, borrowed from Buddhist
philosophy, is that behind or beyond the manifest is the absolute
Void or Emptiness wherein no "thing" essentially exists. Yet there
is no duality in the faintest conceivable form. The Void is a
Plenum-Void; Samsara, the Wheel of Becoming, *is* Nirvana.
There is no need for the inter-position of an outside Reality called
God. Human *is* divine. If there is a God, we are so much part of it
and it of us that there is no difference. Why, then, make use of this
man-made symbol in the sky? John Donne was near to the
Buddhist conception, holding that "God is an angel in an angel,
and a stone in a stone, and a straw in a straw". For, as Dr. Suzuki
points out, "In Zen each individual is an absolute entity, and as
such he is related to all other individuals, and this nexus of infinite
inter-relationships is made possible in the realm of Emptiness
because they all find their being here even as they are, that is, as
individual realities."[1] This and no less is the tremendous theme of
the Buddhist philosophy as developed particularly in the Kegon
School. As he most reasonably adds to the above passage, "This
may be difficult to grasp for those who are not trained to the
Buddhist way of thinking." It is, however, essential to appreciate
that the only philosophy of practical use in Zen is that which is
based on the intuition. The intellect cannot grasp that the Many is
the One without ceasing to be individual things: that the One can

[1] *Zen Buddhism and Its Influence*, p. 220.

be Many and still be One. This is Jijimuge, the complete interfusion of opposites, and, as such, a stage yet higher than the Brahman's 'Thou art THAT', for even in THAT, says the Buddhist, thou art not a whit less thou!

Is Zen atheistic? Yes, if "God" is different from any other form of life which moves to its own enlightenment. "Buddhism is what the world is when you look straight at it," as somebody has said. Why, then, do so through the eyes of an intermediary?

It would, however, be more accurate to say, as Réné Guénon says, that "Buddhism is no more atheistic than it is theistic or pantheistic; all that need be said is that it does not place itself at the point of view where these various terms have any meaning".[1] For we cannot know God intellectually, and when we have learnt to know him, or the Reality of which he is the anthropomorphic dummy, intuitively, we have passed beyond the need of the conception of God. Even reasonably, the God of the Christians is an absurdity in terms of Zen. If he is good then he must be evil; if he is only good he is opposed to evil; in which case there are two things in the Universe, evil and God. If, on the other hand, God is a term for the absolute ultimate All, why chatter about it? "The Tao that can be expressed is not the eternal Tao," and in the same way, "Every statement about the transcendental ought to be avoided because it is invariably a laughable presumption on the part of the human mind, unconscious of its limitations."[2] This is one of the many reasons why Zen hates and strives to avoid abstractions. When a question is put as to the meaning of such terms as Buddha-hood or Reality, the Zen Master invariably turns them down, making the questioner realise that they have no direct hold on life. As an example, the Master Ganto (829-87) was asked, "What is the original, eternal reason?" "Moving," said the Master. "What about it when moving?" asked the questioner. "It is no more the original, eternal reason," replied Ganto, who for once "explained" his reply. "When you assert, you are still in the world of the senses; when you do not assert, you sink into the ocean of birth and death." In Zen affirmation and denial are equal and opposite, and ultimately both are a waste of time. It is, therefore, wise to wipe out the folly of the pursuit of God, and lo! when the pursuit is finally abandoned he will be found waiting in the lounge.

Is Zen, then, a form of mysticism? Have it as you will, for it

---

[1] Quoted in *Diagnosis of Man*, WALKER, p. 184.
[2] *Secret of the Golden Flower*, p. 135.

depends on what is meant by this much-abused and quite exhausted word. There are many forms of mysticism, which Evelyn Underhill defines as the art of union with Reality. Zen would suggest it were better to have tea, being grossly irreverent in the face of vague abstractions. Yet mysticism is a convenient term for the factor which alone gives life and warmth to all religion, and the lack of which makes mere intellectual reasoning such a cold, unprofitable ploy. It is this vision, this self-communion with the vast unconsciousness which lies about the circle of our conscious life, which lifts mere verse into the realm of poetry, fires the imagination, the creative power of the mind, and makes of beauty in all its forms a nobler pursuit than the love of sensuous enjoyment. But it must not be controlled; it must never be fastened or confined. It is "the bloom on the hills at the close of day, the light on the hills at dawn", and if it be fastened to the mind's conception of some extra-cosmic God, though it may produce great poetry, with the Love of the Beloved as a golden refrain, yet it cannot lead to the heart's enlightenment. For still the Lover and the Beloved are two, not one, and even in union there is still not an end. For if all things are reduced to the One, to what is the One reduced? Such mysticism may lift the eyes a long way up the hill, but the Will o' the Wisp of Zen still moves ahead, and its laughter is heard still further up the mountain side.

JIRIKI AND TARIKI

Early Buddhism stressed the necessity of individual effort. "Irrigators guide the water; fletchers straighten arrows; carpenters bend wood; wise men shape themselves." Thus the *Dhammapada*. And again, "Though a man should conquer a thousand times a thousand men in battle, he who conquers himself is the greatest warrior." And again, "By oneself evil is done; by oneself one suffers; by oneself evil is left undone; by oneself one is purified. Purity and impurity are personal concerns. No one can purify another." It is therefore strange that into such a noble and dynamic faith, with its clear command to control and purify the lower man until the last stain of personal desire and its consequent suffering is purged away, there should have crept, as late as the thirteenth century A.D., its very antithesis, the doctrine that effort, however splendid, would never of itself avail, and that faith must supply the deficiency. And the faith was not in the Buddha within, as a guide and teacher, but in Amida, the personified Principle of Buddha-hood who dwelt in a conventional heaven. Only by Tariki, this "other power", could man be saved, and after a while the middle way of Jodo Buddhism, with a balance of Jiriki, "self-power", and Tariki, was replaced by the extreme of Shin Buddhism, wherein all morality and the mind's development was declared to be of no importance so long as faith in Amida was held in the mind and repeated constantly. Thereafter Amida's vow, to save mankind, was sufficient means to Enlightenment, and all who believed would find themselves in the Pure Land of his all-Compassionate Mind. The basic doctrine of early Buddhism, whereby a man is the product of his thoughts and acts and sole creator of his destiny, no God nor all the powers of Heaven having the power to stand between—all this was ended. He who believed would be saved.

If it is argued that faith and love are stronger than the law of Karma, of action-reaction, then it is no law. I prefer the Christian doctrine, "Love is the fulfilling of the law," and regard it as the finer Buddhism. If it be said, and so it was said to me in Japan, that the original doctrine is too hard for the many, then let the many tread, as in other Buddhist countries, so far as they can up the hillside until they are ready for the noble truths of Buddhism. It seems to me wrong to describe this attitude as Buddhism. Of course, there is more to the Buddha's Teaching than this law of moral philosophy, of Karma and rebirth, but the element of love, of a wide compassion for all living things, is no monopoly of the Mahayana, and it is a power that comes, as all comes in the end, from within. "Seek in the impersonal for the Eternal Man, and having sought him out look inward—thou *art* Buddha." True, this spiritual factor, which of course is Zen, may seem to come from without, and so produce an inner experience, or seem to come from within, in which case it will manifest without. But I cannot accept as Buddhism a School which denies the importance of self-development, and nor, I gather, can Dr. Suzuki. "The absolute 'other power' doctrine is not psychologically valid, nor metaphysically tenable." To the extent, therefore, that Zen Buddhism is on one side or other of this Japanese fence, it is undoubtedly Jiriki, moving by "self-power" to its own and the world's enlightenment. There is a well-known story in Zen which may be summarised here. A monk named Dogen, who sought enlightenment, was sent on a very long errand which he thought would interfere with his

studies. Sogen, a fellow monk, took pity on him and agreed to
accompany him. One evening, when Dogen implored his friend to
help him solve the mystery of life, Sogen told him there were five
things which he could not do for his friend—to eat and drink for
him, to respond to the calls of nature for him, and to carry the
"corpse" of his body along the way. Dogen saw the point in a flash,
and attained *satori*. But presumably the truth is some way above
and beyond this pair of opposites. Dr. Suzuki himself has written
of the inner truth of Tariki Buddhism, and is in fact a professor of
the Otani College of the Higashi Hongwanji Temple in Kyoto.
And it was the Prince Abbot of the twin monastery of the Nishi
Hong-wanji in Kyoto who presided, as I have related elsewhere, at
the conference at which I debated this point with his pundits. In
the end he announced, "Mr. Humphreys is right. Tariki and Jiriki
alike are means."[1] And that, as I said in my book, ended the
discussion.

Tariki and Jiriki, then, are both means to an end, another of the
opposites which only exist as such on the plane of discrimination.
But as Zen is itself above such a plane it must exist in both "means"
equally, though its principal vehicle, Zen Buddhism, is unquestion-
ably of the Jiriki School. It is in the degradation of a spiritual truth
that evil lies, in teaching the people that morality and character-
building are of *no* importance. A balance must be obtained, and in
practice I found that it was so in all but the lowest rank of the Pure
Land followers. Thus "Self-hood is revealed in otherness and
otherness in self-hood, which means a complete interpenetration
of subject and object, Amida and his devotees. And we can see that
Buddhism is after all one, and remains so in spite of apparent
diversity."[2]

THE ARHAT AND THE BODHISATTVA IDEAL

The ideal of the Thera Vâda was and is the Arhat, he who by his
own efforts attains Enlightenment. But as the Mahayana
developed, this limited ideal was held to be insufficient. "His
object of spiritual discipline does not extend beyond his own
interest, however exalted it may be in itself—the object being the
attainment of Arhatship, a solitary and saintly life. This is all well
as far as it goes, but as we are all living within a most complicatedly

---

[1] *Via Tokyo* (Hutchinson), p. 74.
[2] *The Eastern Buddhist*, Vol. IV, Pt. 2, p. 32 (of reprint).

organised communal body, not excepting even a Buddha or a Bodhisattva, we have to think of this side of life. The conception of a Bodhisattva was thus inevitable."[1] But is it as simple as all that? "The sages of old got Tao for themselves, then gave it to others," said the Taoist sage, Chuang Tzu. Or, in the words of the *Dhammapada*, "Let a wise man first go the right way himself, then teach others." After all, there is precisely one mind which he can purify, his own; one character to be ennobled, one vision to be widened, his own. How shall he save another from the burning house of desire, that has not saved himself? The change, it would seem, is from depth to width, from the profound study of the few, reaching the whole way to the goal, to a more superficial improvement of the many. As such it may have been an "inevitable conception", but I cannot lightly accept that the Arhat is the less noble ideal. It is, therefore, to be noted that elsewhere Dr. Suzuki modifies his view. "The Arhat and the Bodhisattva are essentially the same, but the Mahayanists, perceiving a deeper sense in Enlightenment as the most important constituent element in the attainment of the final goal of Buddhism, which is spiritual freedom, did not wish to have it operated in themselves only, but wanted to see it realised in every being, sentient and non-sentient."[2] Thus was born the Bodhisattva doctrine which, running as a golden thread through the whole Mahayana, affects Zen Buddhism. The single aim of the Hinayanist became dual. Mahayana stood thereafter on two legs, Maha Prajna, supreme wisdom, and Maha-Karuna, supreme compassion for all living things. Of these Dr. Suzuki says, in a most illuminating phrase, that "the former sees into the unity of things; and the latter appreciates their diversity."[3] He expands this in his latest work, *The Essence of Buddhism*, when talking of Jijimuge. "It is by the Great Compassionate Heart that the Kegon world of Jiji moves. If it were just to reflect one individual Ji after another in the mirror of Ri, the world would cease to be a living one, becoming simply an object of contemplation for the hermit or Arhat. It is the heart indeed that tells us that our own self is a self only to the extent that it disappears into all other selves, non-sentient as well as sentient. ..."[4] This mystical sense of union is, of course, found alike in

[1] *Studies in the Lankâvatâra Sutra*, p. 214.
[2] *Essays I*, p. 52.
[3] *Studies in the Lankâvatâra Sutra*, p. 229.
[4] *The Essence of Buddhism*, p. 55.

eastern and western philosophy. Marcus Aurelius wrote in his diary, "Enter into every man's Inner Self, and let every man enter into thine." And John Donne's famous observation is in the same vein. "Any man's death diminishes me because I am involved in mankind. And therefore never send to know for whom the bell tolls. It tolls for thee."

The Bodhisattva, therefore, at first a name reserved for the few who had neared Nirvana, but later applied to all who vowed to live for the benefit of mankind, was raised as a nobler ideal than that of the Arhat, and the latter was covertly regarded as a selfish aim. Yet "in finding fault with the Hinayanist ideal, the Mahayanist failed to realise that a selfish being could not become an arhatant, which consisted in a spiritual exaltation which transcended the limitations of temporal individuality. In what intelligible sense can a system which aims at the elimination of the phenomenal ego be described as egoistic? . . . The arhatant could not have reached full spiritual development if he had failed to act in accordance with the principle that each man forms a part of a spiritual whole of which all of his fellow men are also parts, and that to serve them is to enrich, while to neglect them is to impoverish, his own higher self."[1]

But whether or not the Arhat is selfish, and whether or not in his narrower objective he avoids the pitfalls of the rival doctrine, including those of over-officiously minding other people's business, the Bodhisattva ideal does liberate the force of compassion. Every monk in a Mahayana monastery recites at intervals the Four Great Vows.

> *"However innumerable sentient beings are*
>   *I vow to save them;*
> *However inexhaustible the passions are*
>   *I vow to extinguish them;*
> *However immeasurable the Dharmas are*
>   *I vow to study them;*
> *However incomparable the Buddha-truth is*
>   *I vow to attain it."*

Thus China and Japan make echo to that noblest of all works of Northern Buddhism, *The Voice of the Silence*. For depth of spiritual feeling and purity of thought it is in a class of its own. Even the Metta Sutta of the Thera Vâda is but the song of human

[1] *Buddhist China*, R. F. JOHNSTON, p. 73.

love as against the "pure serene" of this ancient Tibetan fragment.

"Let thy Soul lend its ear to every cry of pain, like as the lotus bares its heart to drink the morning sun.

Let not the fierce sun dry one tear of pain before thyself has wiped it from the sufferer's eye.

But let each burning human tear drop on thy heart and there remain; nor ever brush it off until the pain that caused it is removed."

"To live to benefit mankind" is the first step on the Path, not the last, in this philosophy, and it is dynamic. "Point out the 'Way'—however dimly, and lost among the host—as does the evening star to those who tread their path in darkness. ... Give light and comfort to the toiling pilgrim, and seek out him who knows still less than thou ... let him hear the Law."

Love is a noble theme, and love itself may be, as Aldous Huxley says, a mode of knowledge, "and when the love is sufficiently disinterested and sufficiently intense, the knowledge becomes unitive knowledge and so takes on the quality of infallibility."[1] There is, indeed, as W. J. Gabb points out, "a kindness of the heart and a kindness of the head. Kindness of the heart prompts us to shake up the pillows of a bed-ridden sufferer, but Jesus told such an one to take up his bed and walk."[2] Love, to be wise, must be lit with Prajna, Wisdom; and Wisdom cannot be complete that is devoid of Love. Thus once more the pair are a pair of opposites and Zen, that seeks not wisdom nor love, both being on the plane of the opposites, drives straight for the state of consciousness which lies beyond all opposites, where Wisdom and Love, Arhat and Bodhisattva, are one—and at the same time what they severally are.

ZEN AND MORALITY

Where is Zen in relation to morality? This is a vague term, having at least two meanings. It may refer to our relations with our fellow men and other forms of life. As such it equates with ethics, and would scarcely obtain if one were alone on a desert island. It may also refer to the inner life of the mind, and equate with character-building, the elimination of low desires and qualities, and their

[1] *The Perennial Philosophy*, p. 95.
[2] From the MS of a lecture.

replacement with nobler qualities. What does Zen have to say about either? Does it take the view of Shin Buddhism at its most extreme, that morality is of no importance so long as the mind be concentrated on the light within? Or does it regard the moral cleansing of the mind as an essential preliminary to further growth? Or does it consider that when the Kingdom of Heaven is attained, all else shall be added unto you—that right morality is the result rather than the cause of *satori,* enlightenment?

It seems that Zen adheres to the doctrine of causation. "As ye sow, so shall ye also reap" is the doctrine known in the East as Karma, action-reaction. Zen, therefore, denies the convenient doctrine of sin-transference, whereby the great ones of the earth apply to those less fortunate, i.e., more lazy, the surplus of their own tremendous merit, acquired from innumerable good deeds. But the law of causation is tempered with compassion, for the love of the loving minds of the earth will affect the incidence of woe, and make the suffering to be borne as the result of folly easier to bear. Moreover, Zen, being of the essence of freedom, resents all rules which hamper and confine the mind. According to Dr. Suzuki, this is one of the reasons for the Japanese preference for art over morality. "Morality is regulative, but art creative. The one is an imposition from without, but the other is an irrepressible expression from within."[1] Zen, he concludes, therefore, finds its inevitable association with art, but not with morality. For rigid form is a symptom of departing life. "When the great Tao is lost, spring forth benevolence and righteousness. When Wisdom and sagacity arise, there are great hypocrites. Where Tao is, equilibrium is. When Tao is lost, out come all the differences of things." This spiritual principle applies specially to the artificial distinctions of "good" and "bad", and Taoism is at least consistent in its philosophy in that it has no moral code. "The Sage has no self (to call his own). He makes the self of the people his self. To the good I act with goodness; to the bad I also act with goodness."[2] Why formulate rules unless the original sense of "right" has been somehow paralysed?

Zen admits that outward conduct must conform with the laws of the State, but the inner life should be above all rules imposed from without. "Definition is always limitation—the 'fixed' and

---

[1] *Zen Buddhism and Its Influence,* p. 21.
[2] *Tao Te Ching,* Chaps. 18 and 49.

THE NATURE OF ZEN BUDDHISM

'changeless' are but terms expressive of a stoppage of growth. People are not taught to be really virtuous, but to behave properly."[1] Yet some degree of discipline is needed, and it is useful so long as it comes from within. It is desire which has to be corrected, not action, for we behave according as we will, and it is an old truth that behind will stands desire. And desire will be purified as the higher, intuitive range of mind increasingly gains control. There is danger in the denial of both good and evil as having real validity, for gross immorality can appear thereby. Zen monasteries are therefore run to a discipline, but it is a control shared willingly, as distinct from a set of rules which most, when occasion offers, will be swift to disobey.

In Zen there is one enemy in the path of final enlightenment, and this is self, the self which stands between a man and the sun while he bitterly complains that it is dark. For self is a knot in the flow of life, an obstruction in the flow of becoming. Life walks on and we strive to prevent it. Yet how bitter our complaint when we are hurt thereby!

A Master was asked, "What is the Way?" "What a fine mountain this is," he said, referring to the mountain where he had his retreat. "I am not asking you about the mountain, but about the Way." "As long as you cannot go beyond the mountain you cannot reach the Way," replied the Master.

The same Master was asked the same question by another monk. "It lies right before your eyes," said the Master.

"Why do I not see it for myself?"

"Because of your egoist notion."

"Do you see it?"

"So long as you have dualist views, saying 'I don't and 'You do', and so on, your eyes are bedimmed by this relativity view."

"When there is neither 'I' nor 'You', can one see it?"

"Where there is neither 'I' nor 'You', who wants to see it?"[2]

The "self" may acquire merit unceasingly by virtuous thoughts and actions, but, as Bodhidharma explained to the Emperor, such merit, though it will by the law of cause-effect improve the character, will have no bearing on the fact of enlightenment. Zen begins where morality leaves off, and its subsequent progress is on a plane where the opposites, like "good" and "bad", have lost their

---

[1] *The Book of Tea*, OKAKURA KAKUZO, p. 53.
[2] *Essays III*, pp. 298-99.

meaning. As Kaiten Nukariya pithily puts it, "Man is not Good-natured or Bad-natured, but Buddha-natured."[1] It is not right conduct, therefore, which matters, but right thinking, thought which springs from the Essence of Mind. Right conduct may be performed in obedience to a moral code, and have no relation to the mind. Right thinking, however, liberated from the illusion of the opposites, will automatically produce "right action", the third step on the Eightfold Path to Enlightenment. "Form and virtue and charity, and duty to one's neighbour, these are accidents of the spiritual," said the Taoist, Chuang Tzu, having in mind, no doubt, the dull Confucian of his day whose life was bound by rigid obedience to an endless code of equally rigid rules.

Zen ethic, therefore, springs from a sense of the unimportance of self, and is fed by the understanding of this fact which flows from the increasing light of enlightenment. Hence the willingness to help all living things to the same liberation of mind. As the Lama said in Talbot Mundy's immortal *Om*, "My son, there is no such thing as sacrifice, except in the imagination. There is opportunity to serve, and he who overlooks it robs himself. Would you call the sun's light sacrifice?"

As a Zen Abbot said to me in Kyoto, "Get Enlightenment; the rest follows"; yet, as Alan Watts points out, "While morality should not be confused with religion, it does take one a certain distance towards the goal; it cannot go the whole way because morality is essentially rigid and limiting, and Zen begins where morality leaves off."[2] Like the intellect, it must be used and then transcended. Meanwhile, perhaps Aldous Huxley should have the last word of all these quotations. "The relationship between moral action and spiritual knowledge is circular, as it were, and reciprocal. Selfless behaviour makes possible an accession of knowledge, and the accession of knowledge makes possible the performance of further and more genuinely selfless actions, which in their turn enhance the agent's capacity for knowing."[3] And so on, until this pair of opposites is merged in Zen.

---

[1] *Religion of the Samurai*, p. 105.
[2] *The Spirit of Zen*, p. 63.
[3] *The Perennial Philosophy*, p. 129.

Chapter 4

In Search of Zen

Asked, "What is Zen?", there is only one truthful answer, "That's it!" For Zen is beyond description. It is the life within form and only a form can be described. It refuses to commit itself to any specified pattern of thinking, to conform to the rules of man's imagining, to fill any mould. "It is a world-power, for in so far as men live at all, they live by Zen."[1] If this be vague it is not the fault of Zen but the fault of the mind's persistent refusal to focus on truth, preferring the forms of truth. Yet Zen, "though far from indefinite, is by itself indefinable because it is the active principle of life itself."[2] Nor is its teaching vague. Coal is black, says Zen. Coal is not black, says Zen. This is clear enough, and both are equally true—or untrue. For Zen slips from the grasp out of either trap, affirmation or denial, both of which limit the boundless, cage the illimitable. Below sense is nonsense, where understanding has not reached the plane of formulated truth. Beyond sense lies non-sense, when the limits of all formulation have been transcended, and only a smile or the lifting of a flower can reveal a shared experience.

Zen is a way of looking at life, a rather unusual way. For it is the direct way, whereby all things are seen just as themselves, and not otherwise, and yet at the same time seen as the interfused aspects of a whole. In Zen all things are ends in themselves, while having no end. To the pure all things are pure; to the Essence of Mind all things just are. And the nearer we are to the Essence of Mind the nearer we are to the things about us which are and yet are not the Essence of Mind. "Consider the lilies of the field, how they grow ...," said Jesus. "Consider the flower in the crannied wall," said Tennyson. Consider anything you please, but just consider it, not as a symbol of eternity, as God in miniature, as a moral lesson or a Great White Hope, but just consider it. "Mysticism uses the object, the finite, as a telescope to look into the infinite. Zen looks at the

[1] BLYTH, *Zen in English Literature*, viii.
[2] *Ibid*, 2.

telescope."[1] As the Master Jimyo said, "As soon as one particle of dust is raised, the great earth manifests itself there in its entirety." It is there, all of it, not symbolically, but actually. There is no need to do more than just to consider it, whatever it may be. The flower is enjoyed for what it is, not otherwise, and he who can rightly look at a flower, without a shadow of ought else intervening, is looking at Zen. Thereafter he is in direct communion with *all* living things, and who shall hate these toes and fingers of his larger self which lie on the mind's periphery? For they are God, if you care to call them so, or Reality, and therefore deserving the gesture which a lover of Zen may pay with the raised hands of respect to a landscape or a noble picture or even to his bowl of tea. Or they are brothers, born of the same father, life, out of the same mother, illusion; or they just are.

For those who prefer the language of modern psychology, he who has achieved this power of direct and therefore illumined vision "is no longer preoccupied with the images of things but merely contains them. The fullness of the world which heretofore pressed upon his consciousness loses none of its richness and beauty, but no longer rules consciousness. The magical claim of things has ceased because the primordial interweaving of consciousness with the world has finally been disentangled. The unconscious is not projected any more, and so the primal *participation mystique* with things is abolished. Therefore, consciousness is no longer preoccupied with compulsive motives but becomes vision. . . . '"[2]

Zen is therefore a matter of experience, and if this has been said many times before, there is little else to be said. It has a subject but no object. It is impersonal, undirected, purposeless. There is no reference in the vast literature of recorded *satori* to union with the Beloved, or to union at all. Zen is a zip-fastener between the opposites. It passes, and they are no more. Yet they are, as none shall deny that once more opens the fastener. Zen is dynamic; it moves and will not wait to be expressed or tethered by the ankle with a phrase. Like Tao,

> *"When one looks at it, one cannot see it;*
> *When one listens to it one cannot hear it;*
> *But when one uses it, it is inexhaustible."*[3]

[1] BLYTH, *Zen in English Literature*, 216.
[2] *Secret of the Golden Flower*, JUNG, pp. 121–22.
[3] *Tao Te Ching*, chap. 35.

Still less can it be the subject of chatter, still less possesed. Said a Master to a pupil who talked about Zen, "You have one trivial fault. You have too much Zen." "But is it not natural for a student of Zen to talk about Zen?" asked the puzzled student. "Why do you hate talking about Zen?" intervened a fellow student. "Because it turns my stomach," said the Master. Well?

Zen has no form, and therefore it has no religion or philosophy of its own. It flowers on a hundred stems, and may use any man-made system to climb to its own integrity. Yet whatever it uses is a substitute for Zen, a mere finger pointing to the moon. No thing, no compound of matter or thought or feeling, must be thought to be the moon when it is but the finger.

Zen is a state of consciousness beyond the opposites. It is also the way to such a condition. It has no form and destroys the forms which are made for it. "Coal is black" may be true. So, says Zen, is the opposite, that coal is not black. Both statements limit the truth by an intellectual equation between two things of relative existence. Do we KNOW the coal any more by sticking upon it the label, "black"?

Yet the mind is partial to clothing for truth, being somewhat prudish about her essential nakedness. Even Bodhidharma is said to have laid down the four fundamental principles already set out. Let us consider them.

A SPECIAL TRANSMISSION OUTSIDE THE SCRIPTURES

Is Zen, then, esoteric? Some say yes, that in fact it never had an exoteric form. The Robe was handed down from Patriarch to Patriarch, and for a long time nothing of this "transmission" was written down. In the Samyutta Nikaya of the Pali Canon is the famous story of the simsapa leaves. Taking up a handful of leaves, the Buddha asked his disciples, "What think ye, Brethren, which are the more, these leaves that I hold in my hand or those in the grove above?" The inevitable answer being given, he made his point. "Just so, those things that I know but have not revealed are greater by far than those that I have revealed. . . . And why have I not revealed them? . . . Because they do not conduce to profit, are not concerned with the holy life. . . ." To those who have need of words to communicate experience, there is a limit to what may be taught with profit. Yet those who have opened the "third eye" of the intuition may speak with the Master on his own exalted plane.

A Confucian came to a Master to be initiated into Zen. The Master quoted Confucius, "Do you think I am holding something back from you? Indeed, I have held nothing back!" The Confucian was about to answer, when the Master thundered, "No!" The enquirer was troubled in his mind, but later, when walking in the mountains with the Master, they passed the wild laurel in bloom, and the air was redolent. "Do you smell it?" asked the Master. "There,"he said, when the Confucian agreed, "I have kept back nothing from you!"

There is, therefore, a transmission outside the Scriptures, yet these Scriptures form a remarkable body of literature. All alike must be read with the intuition. "They are direct expressions of spiritual experience, they contain intuitions gained by digging down deeply into the abyss of the Unconscious, and they make no pretension of presenting them through the mediumship of the intellect."[1] None is canonical in the sense that it is authoritative, for Buddhism knows no authority. The most used Scriptures are the *Lankâvatâra Sutra*, bequeathed to the fold of Zen by Bodhidharma; the *Diamond Sutra*, the hearing of which converted the 6th Patriarch Hui-neng; the *Sutra of Hui-neng (Wei Lang)* himself, and perhaps the *Huang-Po Doctrine of Universal Mind*. All these are available in English. Portions of the *Avatamsaka Sutra*, described by Dr. Suzuki as the consummation of Buddhist thought and Buddhist experience, appear in Mrs. Suzuki's *Mahayana Buddhism*. In Zen monasteries in Japan the *Prajnaparamitahridaya Sutra* (the Shingyo), being short, is recited on all occasions; the *Kwannon Sutra*, the Japanese name for the Samantamukha-parivarta, appears very frequently. But all these are, as Kaiten Nukariya calls them, "religious currency representing spiritual wealth". They are substitutes, at the best, for actual experience. Indeed, the scorn of the Zen practitioner for the printed word has at times been carried too far. Even the ability to read and write has been frowned upon, and the utmost ignorance of normal affairs been praised as a virtue. This is the folly of extremes, like the burning of books. Though the finger points to the moon and is not the moon, it is foolish to ignore the finger until the way to the moon is clear. Even if "the Universe is the Scripture of Zen", as Mr. Nukariya insists, there are volumes in which its learning is made more immediately available. Yet "the man who

[1] *Essays*, III, p. 7.

talks much of the Teaching but does not practise it, is like a cowman counting another's cattle; he is no disciple of the Blessed One";[1] or, in the later words of Hui-neng, "Whether Sutra-reciting will enlighten you or not depends on yourself. He who recites the Sutra with the tongue and puts its teaching into actual practice with the mind 'turns round' the Sutra. He who recites it without putting it into practice is 'turned round' by the Sutra."[2]

NO RELIANCE UPON WORDS OR LETTERS

This seems but an extension of the first, almost the antiphonal principle of the Psalms. Yet it rubs the lesson in. Words are but marks on paper or noises in the air. At the best they are symbols for the truth, substitutes, and poor ones, for another's experience. "Those who know do not speak; those who speak do not know," says the *Tao Te Ching*, "yet words are needed to transcend words, and intellection is needed to rise above the intellect, except that this rising must not be made in a dualistic or 'escapist' sense, for no such escape is here possible."[3] Words are the pins on which the butterflies of life are stuck to a board. They may look pretty, but their *raison d'être* has gone. Words exist for their meaning, of which they are but the shadow, and if they enshrine some part of the meaning, they probably obscure still more. Hence the Zen search for other and better ways to convey experience. These methods, a shout, a blow, a joke, a paradox or gesture, silence itself, are more direct as a medium, and "this medium functions 'directly' and 'at once' as if it were the experience itself—as when deep calls to deep. This direct functioning is compared to one brightly burnished mirror reflecting another which stands facing the first with nothing in between".[4]

Some "devices" are frowned upon in Zen. Images have their value as a focus point for concentration and for the paying of respect to the memory of the Teacher whose Enlightenment is Zen. But not otherwise.

When the Master Tanka was bitterly cold he took a wooden image from the shrine of the temple where he was staying and put it in the fire. The keeper of the shrine was not unnaturally horrified.

---

[1] *Dhammapada*, v. 19.
[2] *Sutra of Wei Lang*, pp. 70–71.
[3] *The Essence of Buddhism*, p. 26.
[4] DR. SUZUKI in *Philosophy, East and West*, p. 113.

But Tanka was poking about in the ashes with his stick. "What are you looking for?" asked the keeper. "The holy '*sariras*'," said the Master, referring to the relics said to be found in the ashes of a saint. "But there aren't any in a wooden Buddha," said the keeper. "Then give me the other two images," said Tanka.

Zen is indeed iconoclastic. "Do not linger where the Buddha is, and where he is not, pass on." When Joshu found a monk in the temple worshipping the image of the Buddha he struck him with his staff. "Is there not anything good in the worship of the Buddha?" asked the monk. "Nothing is better than anything good," was the famous reply.

DIRECT POINTING TO THE SOUL OF MAN

Zen points, and is what is pointed at. This "soul" or *hsin,* the Chinese word which covers inmost heart or mind, is the Tao of the Taoist; to the Buddhist, the Buddha within. All that points to it points truly, and according to Zen all things are fingers pointing to the same experience. The way is clear enough; it is a process of dropping the veils which we hold in front of us, all of them, not a carefully selected few. "Straightforwardness is the holy place, the Pure land," said Hui-neng, quoting the *Vimalakirti Nirdesa Sutra.* And between the two ends of straightforwardness nothing at all must intervene. Speaking of the folly of definition, a monk asked a Master, "Am I right when I have no idea?" Jyoshu, the Master, answered, "Throw away that idea of yours." "What can I throw away?" asked the monk. "You are free, of course, to carry about that useless idea of no idea." The monk, it is said, was enlightened. Then why, if this be true, do we need a library of books wherewith to find ourselves? For fifteen hundred years Zen Masters have "pointed" without them and, as Dr. Suzuki asks, "when a syllable or a wink is enough, why spend one's life in writing huge books, or building a grandiose cathedral?"[1] (All right—I know, but this is my way of *learning* Zen.)

SEEING INTO ONE'S OWN NATURE

This nature is *hsin,* the personal veil which hides from us the Essence of Mind. It is everywhere and everything, and when anything is suddenly seen for what it is, then *hsin* is seen, and Zen.

[1] *The Eastern Buddhist,* Vol. VI, p. 121.

Pointing to a stone in front of his temple, To-shi said, "All the
Buddhas of the past, the present and the future are living therein."
But this would not have stopped him using the stone as a hammer
to crack nuts. When Tennyson plucked the flower from the
crannied wall and held it in his hand he realised, "But if I could
understand what you are, root and all, and all in all, I should know
what God and man is." But, as R. H. Blyth points out, a Zen
Master might take the flower and crush it and ask, "*Now* do you
know what God and man is?"[1] For the crushing of the flower is like
the burning of the text-book; it destroys the last veil, in this case of
sentiment, which hid from the poet the essence of the flower.
Things, in brief, are not symbols, but things, and the whole of
Samsara, the manifested Universe, is only the Essence of Mind in
reverse. See it "right" and it is One, though none the less a rose, or a
committee meeting, or a pint of beer. Such is the nature of things,
and "This Nature is the Mind, and the Mind is the Buddha, and the
Buddha is the Way, and the Way is Zen. To see directly into one's
original Nature, this is Zen."[2]

What are the symptoms of awakening Zen? They are many, and
may be better considered in the chapter relating to Satori. Yet here
are three.

There is, first, an increasing serenity, however disturbed at times
by the usual gusts of emotion or doubt. There is a sense of
certainty, not boastful or aggressive in manifestation, but
peaceful, as of a ship which, storm-tossed in a sea still visible, now
lies safe-harboured while the storm howls overhead. There is a
withdrawal of interest from the manifold means of escape from
Reality in which we pass our lives, an increasing intensity of
purpose and awareness which yet has lost to a large extent the
quality of tension. There is a sense of airiness, of the lightness
which comes of dropping the burden of self and its desires, of the
health and vigour of youth on the uplands of new thought in the
dawn-light of the world. There is a sense of returning, a feeling of
having recovered the natural simplicity of life which springs from
the rediscovery of our Essence of Mind. There is even a sense of
inconsequence, from understanding of the relative unimportance
of habitual affairs. Yet at the same time there is a growing
awareness of the significance of things and events, impersonal
now, but immediate. The humblest act is a sacrament, the

[1] BLYTH, *Zen in English Literature*, p. 68.
[2] *Essays* I, p. 220.

humblest thing, mind-made though it is, is now of absolute value. There is, in brief, an increasing sense of balance, a refusal to rest the mind in any of the pairs of opposites, a refusal, indeed, to let the mind rest anywhere at all.

This firm refusal comes from a new-born sense of flow. Asked, "What is Zen?", a Master replied, "Walk on!" For life is like a river, filling each form and bursting its limitations as it moves unceasing on. It is therefore useless to sit down in achievement, or in any concept, even "Zen". Hsin (in Japanese, shin) becomes mu-shin, "no mind", for who shall confine the sunset or the morning wind in a labelled box of thought, however splendid its construction and design? Speaking of Hui-neng, Dr. Suzuki writes, "The Mind of Self-Nature was to be apprehended in the midst of its working or functioning. The object of dhyâna (Zen) was thus not to stop the working of Self-Nature but to make us plunge right into its stream and seize it in the very act. His intuitionalism was dynamic. . . ."[1] For "the truth of Zen is the truth of life, and life means to live, to move, to act, not merely to reflect. Is it not the most natural thing for Zen, therefore, that its development should be towards acting or rather living its truth instead of demonstrating or illustrating its truth in words, that is to say, with ideas? In the actual living of life there is no logic, for life is superior to logic. . . . Zen is to be explained, if explained it should be, rather dynamically than statically. When I raise the hand thus, there is Zen. But when I assert that I have raised the hand, Zen is no more there".[2] "Be prepared," say the Boy Scouts, echoing Hamlet's

> "If it be now, 'tis not to come; if it be not to come
> It will be now; if it be not now, yet it will come:
> The readiness is all."

Hence the value of what Geraldine Coster calls "Sitting loose to life", a fluid adaptability to unyielding circumstance, attached to nothing, experiencing all.

> "He who bends to himself a joy
> Doth the wingéd life destroy;
> But he who kisses the Joy as it flies,
> Lives in eternity's sunrise."

Security, to many the principal purpose of life, is seen to be as

---

[1] *Essays* I, p. 207.
[2] *Ibid*, pp. 283–84.

undesirable as it is impossible of attainment. Emily Dickenson is right.

> *"In insecurity to lie*
> *Is Joy's insuring quality."*

In brief, without thought of security or achievement, or any purpose, much less an ultimate goal, "Walk on!"

A third of the many symptoms of awakening Zen, and the last to be mentioned here, is a sense of "rightness". "All that happens happens right," said the Emperor Marcus Aurelius. "I know that the enterprise is worthy. I know that things work well. I have heard no bad news." Thus Thoreau, and they are brave and splendid words. From the first experience of Zen is born a willingness to let things happen, a diminishing desire to control the universe, even though the purpose be to "rebuild it, nearer to the heart's desire". Action becomes increasingly "right action", done without haste or delay, without thought of self, without thought of merit or reward.

> *"He who pursues learning will increase every day.*
> *He who pursues Tao will decrease every day.*
> *He will decrease and continue to decrease*
> *Till he comes to non-action;*
> *By non-action everything can be done."*[1]

Yet herein lies the paradox of personality. As self dies out, the true self grows. Of the Tao or Zen it is later said,

> *"When merits are accomplished it does not lay claim to*
> *them.*
> *Because it does not lay claim to them, therefore it does*
> *not lose them."*[2]

The secret lies in action in inaction, or inaction in action, as explained at length in the Bhagavad Gita. Deeds are done because it is "right" to do them, regardless of consequence, and merit, the results of right action which accrue to the doer as long as there is a "doer" to receive them, is a by-product which comes, like happiness, unsought.

Yet the habit of right action is itself presumably the result of previous lives of merit-producing action, by which the mind, increasingly lightened of the weight of personal desire, is slowly

[1] *Tao Te Ching*, Chap. 48.
[2] *Ibid*, Chap. 51.

enlarged by the deliberate expansion, in range and depth, of its activity. I found in *The Westminster Problems Book* (1908) a delightful quatrain by Philip Castle which puts this admirably.

GOOD TASTE

> *"Merit acquired in incarnations past,*
> *And now by the unconscious self held fast;*
> *So the hand strikes the right chord, in the dark,*
> *And, codeless, runs the right flag to the mast."*

For the law of Karma, action-reaction, operates unceasingly as long as a self exists to receive the consequences, "good" or "bad", of action. Hence the advice in *The Voice of the Silence*: "Follow the wheel of life; follow the wheel of duty to race and kin, to friend and foe, and close thy mind to pleasures as to pain. Exhaust the law of karmic retribution. . . ." And the law can only be exhausted, as already set out, by exhausting the self-ish desires which keep alive the separate, personal self.

Buddhism in the East is known as the Buddha-Dharma (Pali: Dhamma). The word Dharma has a vast variety of meanings, one of which is "duty". But duty in English has the unpleasant connotation of compulsion. It is something which ought to be done but which, generally speaking, we do not wish to do. Yet in the Buddhist sense it is that which is the next thing to be done, and the emotional labels of dislike or like are not applied. One just does it. In a memorable passage Chuang Tzu begins, "To act by means of inaction is Tao. To speak by means of inaction is exemplification of Tao." It ends, "To follow Tao is to be prepared. (Cp. "The readiness is all".) And not to run counter to the natural bias of things is perfect."[1] This "natural bias of things" is the rhythm of nature, the rhythm of the Universe. "It connotes acting in harmony with the swing of the Universe—whether spiritually, intellectually or in the least movement of the body—from the physical movements of the dance of happy youth to the dance of the planets about the sun and the systems about the infinite."[2] Alan Watts has much to say of this in *The Meaning of Happiness*. Talking of the Taoist conception of the significance of the moment, he says that this implies that all things happening now have a definite relation to one another just because they have

[1] CHUANG TZU, p. 137.
[2] *The Story of Oriental Philosophy*, ADAMS BECK, p. 413.

occurred together in time, if for no other reason. This is another way of saying that there is a harmony called Tao which blends all events in each moment of the Universe into a perfect chord. The whole situation in and around you at this instant is a harmony with which you have to find your own union if you are to be in accord with Tao. The right life, therefore, is the natural life, and he who has found and lives in Zen lives naturally. To what extent his new found harmony affects his outward life, to bring his outward mode of living into accord with his inner awareness, is a matter of time and the individual, but just as the direct drive of an engine is sweet and without discordant tension, so the right use of action, direct action, is sweet and frictionless. Only self, the desire of self for self, intervenes and pulls the machine out of alignment. Alignment becomes the operative word. From the "power-house of the Universe" as Trine calls it, to the individual self the power is direct, and the right means used in the right way at the right time and place makes up increasingly the perfect act.

A sense of serenity, a sense of flow, and a sense of rightness in all action, these are three of the symptoms of awakening Zen, and the number of men in whom such a state of awareness flowered in China and Japan between the sixth and the nineteenth centuries produced in their outward influence what may be fairly called the visible fruits of Zen, as manifest in Zen Buddhism.

Chapter 5

The Fruits of Zen

"By their fruits ye shall know them." Zen is to Zen Buddhism as life to form, but as the life is formless it is by the visible form that one must judge the quality and value of the life. What is the record of Zen Buddhism, what its effect on the people of China and Japan, their life and culture, art and philosophy?

ZEN INFLUENCE IN CHINA

The impact of Zen upon the Chinese character was tremendous, and none the less so for the fact that its form-side is in a way the product of that character. As already explained, the Buddhism which first arrived in China was indigestible to the Chinese mind, and it was only after centuries of adaptation that it became an expression of their highest thought. The Chinese from the dawn of history have shown themselves a practical people, with a love of beauty, the beauty of worldly things, which is almost a religion in itself. As early as the third millennium B.C. their art, so far as we know it, was complex and advanced in form, noble and serene in character, and it is idle to suggest that its highest flowering, in the T'ang Dynasty (A.D. 618—906) and the Sung Dynasties (A.D. 960—1279), was of purely Buddhist origin. But none who has studied the subject denies that the great outpouring of the creative art which occurs soon after the founding of Zen Buddhism was lit by the flame of Zen. Here was art at its noblest, the attempt of man to express the vision of a world beyond the opposites. "The followers of Zen aimed at direct communion with the inner nature of things, regarding their outward accessories only as impediments to a clear perception of Truth."[1] To this extent the memory of the metaphysical philosophy of Indian Buddhism persisted in China. Speaking of Chinese æstheticism, and in particular of Chinese goddesses, Mr. J. W. G. Mason, after quoting the Chinese saying, "Fulfilment is deception", says "The created thing, woman in her

[1] *The Book of Tea*, p. 62.

normal, living role, does not provoke the æsthetic ecstasy. Feminism in the abstract, not in woman's individual reality but so idealised as to be a continual fount of æsthetic suggestiveness, is the desire".[2] So with every "thing". It is the process of creation, not the created thing, which excites the Chinese mind. All things are subject to Sunyata, the Plenum-Void which underlies all manifestation. In the end, "the knower becomes the object of his knowledge, the artist the thing he visions or conceives, and if he possesses the proper means of exteriorisation, he will transmit in symbols or shapes or signs something which contains a spark of that eternal stream of life or consciousnes which abides when forms decay."[2] There is in the art of T'ang and Sung no sign of copying, either from nature herself or from another age. The inspiration bubbles straight from the living rock. Nature is not an enemy to be conquered or harnessed, as in the West, but a friend with whom to blend one's soul in exquisite communion. "We never grow tired of one another, the mountain and I," said the Chinese poet, Li-Po. The use of rhythm and the use of space are hall-marks of great Chinese art. By "rhythm" is meant that conscious—one might say super-conscious—co-operation with the forces of life, or nature. "The idea that art is the imitation of nature is altogether foreign to Eastern painters. Their work is to create, and not to imitate or copy. The special merit of a picture is to be sought in its spiritual rhythm and not in its composition, in its invisible atmosphere and not in its visible forms"[3] And space, to the Chinese artist, is not mere absence of form. It is dynamic. As it is written in the *Tao Te Ching* (Chapter XI),

> "*Doors and windows are cut in the walls of a house,*
> *And because they are empty spaces, we are able to use*
> *   them.*
> *Therefore on the one hand we have the benefit of*
> *   existence*
> *And on the other, we make use of non-existence.*"

"To make use of non-existence," this to the Chinese artist is an everyday affair, and the "one-corner" art of those painters who left the greater part of their pictures blank was not mere cleverness.

[1] *The Creative East*, p. 69.
[2] "Ch'an (Zen) Buddhism and its Relation to Art", OSVALD SIREN, in *The Theosophical Path*, October, 1934, p. 169.
[3] *Essays*, III, p. 342.

These artists were using non-existence in a work of art created in existence, and they thereby lifted the mind of the beholder to the plane of their own experience.

Finally, Zen art is an individual art. It may be objected that all art is individual, and so in a way it is. But the inspiration of Zen art is Zen, a state of consciousness beyond the opposites, a state of serene, detached awareness of eternal things or, to be less poetic and more accurate, of the eternal quality in all things as they are. And this awareness is personal, so personal that it cannot be described, much less taught in class. It follows that Zen Buddhism, and indeed all Buddhism, ignores the mass. The Eightfold Path of the Blessed One is a Noble (Aryan) Path for noble minds; though available to the many it can never at any time be trodden by more than the few. The Bodhisattva may work for all mankind, but it is each of all mankind which in the end must make the effort for self-deliverance. "The hope of mankind does not lie in the action of any corporate body, be it ever so powerful, but in the influence of individual men and women who for the sake of a greater have sacrificed a lesser aim."[1] The mass, by whatever name described, makes nothing except trouble for the individual. As C. G. Jung points out, "'Society' is nothing more than a concept of the symbiosis of a group of human beings. A concept is not a carrier of life. The sole and natural carrier of life is the individual, and this holds true throughout nature."[2]

The variety of expression was enormous, and how could it be otherwise? For the inspiration came from the centre and worked outwards, and whether it appeared in large or small design, in sculpture, ivory or bronze, in pictures, poems or buildings, was a matter of choice for the artist-creator. In the same way, it appears in different forms in different countries. "Just because (Zen) teaches inwardness and nothing else," says Keyserling, "it has produced profoundly different results among nations of different temperaments. ... Its Indian disciples were made more profound in recognition. In China it led to a unique revival of feeling for nature; the greatest masters of landscape painting were all adepts in Zen. In Japan it became the central school for heroism. ..."[3]

[1] *Diagnosis of Man*, KENNETH WALKER, p. 219.
[2] *Essays on Contemporary Events*, p. 31.
[3] *Travel Diary of a Philosopher*, II, p. 228.

ZEN INFLUENCE IN JAPAN

Buddhism reached Japan, as already described, in the seventh century, but Zen Buddhism, derived from the Ch'an Sect of China, only became a powerful influence in the Kamakura period of the thirteenth century. Thereafter its effect in depth and range was immense. "The difficulty the West experiences in understanding Japanese civilisation is due primarily to the strange spectacle of a spiritual, æsthetic and utilitarian evolution progressing as a single nationalistic movement."[1] For, as the author points out, the West still inclines to look upon these three as independent factors of life, to be kept apart rather than united, lest they contaminate each other. Yet in the East these things are seen as aspects of one whole, and this united vision is, in itself, to some extent, the effect of Zen.

Certainly the range of effect was vast. As Steinilber-Oberlin writes, "The same foundation of Buddhist purity allows the Zenist to become a monk, a poet or a knight, to acquire an enterprising and acceptant soul, because the secret of these different states is absolute detachment and intuitive originality. Zen is not the metaphysics of an exhausted mind; it is a vigorous activity of the soul."[2] And Sir George Sansom, in an oft-quoted passage, says, "The influence of the Zen School upon Japan has been so subtle and pervading that it has become the essence of her finest culture. To follow its ramifications in thought and sentiment, in art, letters and behaviour, would be to write exhaustively the most difficult and the most fascinating chapter of her spiritual history...."[3]

The secret of it all is that indefinable virtue which is known as *wabi* or *sabi*. *Wabi* is described as "poverty", or "aloofness", a state of mind which is satisfied with few possessions, and is untied to worldly affairs. This state, needless to say, is compatible with the actual possession of chattels, or the holding of office. It is a chastity of heart unstained by the circumstance in which it moves, in which it finds experience. *Sabi* (Sanskrit: *Santi*) may, I think, be described as the application of *wabi* to art. Much has been written by experts on the spirit of Japanese art. It is impersonal in the highest sense; it is of the people in its range of sensuous appeal, yet never for one moment sensual; it is purposeless, like nature in her myriad manifestations, and leads to, as it is the outcome of, a love of nature which is one of the noblest products of Japan. The artist

[1] *The Creative East,* MASON, p. 101.
[2] *The Buddhist Sects of Japan,* p. 138.
[3] *Japan,* p. 338.

strives to achieve results with the minimum display, be it number of brush strokes in a picture, rocks in a garden or flowers in a vase. In the same way a Japanese house is the loveliest product of Japan. Nowhere in the world is such utter chastity of taste, so much achieved of beauty and comfort with the minimum means. A Japanese room is all but empty, as the mind should be of thoughts, and beauty and truth and quietude have room in which to live. There is here no following of the rules of art. Each artist, using the term in its widest possible sense, must move from the centre of his being out to the manifestation of that inward Essence of Mind. Georges Duthuit's description of the way in which a Chinese artist paints bamboos is rightly famous. "Draw bamboos for ten years, become a bamboo, then forget all about bamboos when you are drawing. In possession of an infallible technique, the individual places himself at the mercy of inspiration."[1] Nor is this a mere flight of fancy by the author concerned. In an article in the *Bulletin of Eastern Art* (which I discovered, forgotten by the author, in the depths of his library at Kamakura), Dr. SUZUKI describes how the creator of the famous dragon ceiling in the monastery of Myosin-Ji, the headquarters of the Rinzai sect of Zen in Kyoto, achieved his task. He wished the dragon to be realistic, in a terrifying degree, and, barren of method, finally approached the Abbot of the monastery, a great Zen Master of his day. The Master's advice was simple: "Become the dragon." And so it was painted.

But the subject of Zen in art is enormous, and here there is but room to touch upon its main effects on Bushido and the cult of the sword, on the arts of the Tea Ceremony, gardening, dress and the like, and on the life in a Zen monastery.

Bushido, the cult of knighthood which dominated the Middle Ages of Japan, was a blend of Shinto, Confucianism and Buddhism, and the last element was largely Zen. It is a warrior cult, demanding self-discipline, self-abnegation, contempt of pain and suffering, and the most tremendous will to achieve the moment's aim. So is Zen; hence its immediate popularity with the Samurai class. "Its simplicity, directness and efficiency instantly won the heart of the warrior, and the samurais began to knock at the monastery gate."[2] Both have an absolute contempt of death, for both, before becoming proficient, have already experienced it. This (subjective) experience is one of the most remarkable

[1] Quoted in Dr. Suzuki's *Zen Buddhism and its Influence*, p. 26.
[2] *The Zen Sect of Buddhism*, p. 26.

products of Zen. Yet if things, whether tangible possessions or fruits of the mind, have already been surrendered, what can death, that rest between two earthly lives, remove that is of value? Nor is the idea entirely strange to western ears. One Englishman has held it and magnificently phrased it. Shakespeare, in one of the finest of his sonnets, says:

> *"Poor soul, the centre of my sinful earth,*
> *. . . live thou upon thy servant's loss,*
> *And let that pine to aggravate thy store;*
> *Buy terms divine in selling hours of dross;*
> *Within be fed, without be rich no more:*
> *So shalt thou feed on death that feeds on men,*
> *And death once dead, there's no more dying then."*

Kendo, the fencing with a two-handed sword, carries on the same tradition, for the leading fencers of the day still wear their lives as the Samurai wore his swords, lightly yet with honour and with dignity. Their spirit of attack is tremendous, and the speed of action is such that he who pauses to think would be, were his opponent's sword of steel, most neatly severed in two. According to the famous precepts of Takuan, the most important factor in Kendo is "Immovable wisdom", an intuitive state in which all is in motion save the inmost centre of the mind. This is Zen, for nothing could be more "direct" than the line of motion—ahead. "That the Japanese sword is to be used with both hands and that the Japanese warrior never carries a shield, show how well the Samurai appreciates the practice of Zen, in which the idea of 'going-straight-ahead-ness' is strongly emphasised."[1] Judo, the modern term for Jiu-Jitsu, is even more the application of Zen principles. It is, indeed, the Taoist *wu-wei* in action, for the power used is one's opponent's power, turned to his own undoing, and the victor wins by giving way. Here is no pitting of strength to strength : a girl can throw, and I have watched it a hundred times, a man nearly twice her size, for she marries her skill to his movement, and it is with his own force that he hits the mats with such a resounding thud. For myself, I knew the meaning of Zen for the first time on the night when, without "thought" or feeling, I leapt to opportunity and in the fraction of time that my opponent was off his balance, threw him directly, cleanly, utterly. Japanese

[1] *Training of the Zen Buddhist Monk*, p. ix.

art and culture is a very wide term, but wherever one looks in this most lovely field, one sees the light of Zen.

A Japanese house, and all within and about it, shows such chastity of taste as is only the product of a most refined and lovely mind, and the *tokonoma*, the alcove-shrine in the living-room, which holds but a single picture and a single vase of flowers, is derived from the Buddhist altar before which the Samurai of old drank ritual tea to Bodhidharma, that spiritual warrior who showed the way to Zen. And the Zen garden of Ryoanji, admittedly a technique carried to extremes, what can the West derive from a waste of white sand, the size of a tennis lawn, and in it but five groups of rock? Yet the rocks are placed so perfectly, so "right", that the heart is satisfied as though with a burden of flowers, and the whole effect, as I murmured to myself when I first saw it, is best compared to unaccompanied Bach. In the words of Laurence Binyon, "that singular garden of Soami's, with its nakedness, its abstraction, shows the Zen spirit in an extreme form. In the art inspired by Zen all the emphasis is on the interior life, and the communication of ideas is reduced to the simplest, barest forms. It is an art of suggestion rather than expression."[1] The same applies to Japanese flower-arrangement, no bud nor leaf too many and each perfect of its kind, and to the beauty and neatness of their national dress. It applies to their poetry, of which more later, to *sumiye* painting, and above all to Cha-no-yu, the Tea Ceremony. I have attempted, in my *Via Tokyo* to describe this exquisite lay sacrament of friends, and have no more to say. Okakura Kakuzo, in his famous *Book of Tea*, calls it the adoration of the beautiful amongst everyday facts. It is more than that. The "ceremony" is simple enough; the water is boiled, the tea is made, those present drink it and the bowls are then washed up and dried. But every movement in the entire performance is pre-ordained, rehearsed and perfectly performed. The making and drinking of tea has no objective value; all depends on the state of mind, and the state of mind is Zen. What a relief for the warriors of old to leave their swords at the entrance of the tiny, empty, and exquisitely simple tea-house, and to rest their minds in the Void of pure abstraction expressed in a perfect mind-less ritual, in which they use and handle homely, simple things.

And all these forms of art are virile in the extreme. It was no more "soft" for a warrior to join in the making of tea, or the swift

[1] *The Spirit of Man in Asian Art*, p. 144.

composition of a poem or painting, than it was for a Rajput prince, with a wrist of steel for a sword, to be lord of a large harem and a connoisseur in scent. For Zen is life, vigorous and virile life, and none the less so because it may be expressed in a gentle, feminine form.

Even more is the spirit of Zen made manifest in the monastery temples of Japan. As already stated, it is in Japan that Zen can best be studied, and although there are three sects of Zen, the Rinzai, Soto and Obaku, there is little difference between them. The temple sites are various. Some, as in Kyoto, are in the heart of great cities; some are deep in the country. Most, however, are near enough to a town to serve its needs and yet to be free of its importunity. The country sites are always, as in China, exquisitely chosen, and the spacious dignity of the whole demesne, with its various buildings carefully placed, and the whole set about with pines or cryptomerias through which the tones of the great bronze bell flood softly, night and day, is a profound experience which neither the senses nor the home-sick heart can ever quite forget.

The heart of the monastery is the Zen-Do, the Meditation Hall, wherein the younger monks both work and sleep, and all assemble daily. To this extent the Zen sect is the Meditation sect of Japanese Buddhism, but the meditation practised therein is far from the contemplation of the abstract usually implied in the term. There is here no Indian Yoga, no development of the Siddhis, the spiritual powers which all possess but which are dormant in the average mind. Nor is there Bhakti Yoga, the devotion to the Beloved which purifies and lifts the emotions to a higher plane; nor is there Karma Yoga as a deliberate exercise, though the outcome of even the lower stages of satori is to produce "right action", in the sense of the Bhagavad Gita, whereby "the perfect act has no result". The Zen-Do is the home of the *koan* exercise, the concentration of mind and heart and will on the breaking of the bonds of the intellect, that the light of the intuition may illumine the mind, and the domination of the opposites be broken once and for all.

The life of the monks encourages three virtues: simplicity, purity in the sense of spiritual poverty, and the cult of beauty as a faculty of the mind, and all are plainly visible. Their persons, their homes and the monastery grounds are scrupulously clean; possessions are cut to a minimum; their whole life is a round of cheerful, strenuous effort in most beautiful surroundings wherein the whole of the man is directed, fiercely and utterly, to one end, satori, the attainment of direct, im-mediate awareness of the world of non-discrimination wherein the stream of life runs joyously and boundlessly and free.

Comparison with a western "priest" is obvious. The Zen monks take no vows; they may leave their particular monastery or the monastic life at will. They marry, and the minor temples within the greater curtailage are alive with the adorable children of Japan. There are no mortifications, for Zen is an attitude to life, not disgust with it; an escape into life, not an escape from it. There is no worship in the western sense, for the Buddha, whether as man or as the spirit of Buddha-hood, is already one with the worshipper, and all men know it. For Zen is the spirit of man, and as such it cannot be added to, nor can anyone take from it away. The Zen monk is never, therefore, an intermediary between God and man, if only for the excellent reason that Zen knows nothing of God. Each monastery has a spiritual and secular director, sometimes the same man, often different. But even the Roshi (Zen Master) is no nearer God than a blade of grass; he is only nearer to his own enlightenment. And as each man is already, though he "knows" it not, enlightened, how should he need the services of any other man to enlighten him, or to save him from the consequences, "good" or "evil", of his acts?

All monks work. "No work, no food!" said the Master Hyakujo, and for a thousand years the monks of Zen have obeyed him. They receive an all-round training, physical as well as spiritual, for in Zen the two are one. Ploughing a field or peeling potatoes is to them as divine as the daily service in the Hon-Do or main temple, and whether the work be of body or mind it is done with the utmost effort. "Unless at one time perspiration has streamed down your back, you cannot see the boat sailing before the wind," said a Master of the *koan* exercise, and the same applies to a day in the fields. Whether working with his hands or his mind, the effort is high and continuous. "You yourself must make the effort; Buddhas do but point the way," says the *Dhammapada*. And again, "What has to be done, do with determination. The lazy monk merely scatters the dust of passion more widely." It needs high purpose to achieve purposelessness, and there is nothing gentle about the discipline of Zen, as the conventional portraits of Bodhidharma show. When a man wants Zen as fiercely and whole-heartedly as he wants air when his head is being held under water, he may find it, but not before! When a student complained that the

Master would not talk to him, the Master replied, "An earnest student of Zen begrudges the time even to trim his nails; how much more the time wasted in conversation with others!" In Buddhism "meditation is an act of attention, an effort of will. It is not passive reverie but intense striving, concentration of mind in which will and thought become fused. According to Buddha's teaching each man will have to find salvation, in the last resort, alone and with his own will, and he needs all the will in the world for so formidable an effort."[1] Mindful and self-possessed at all times, the Zen monk does each act deliberately, or does not do it at all. His whole day is a hard day's work at the task of enlightenment, for himself and all mankind.

The Japanese love of nature is proverbial, and the perfect siting of the temples, and the gardens which surround each dwelling, feed that love. All is beautifully kept; nothing is wasted. He who uses a tool must use it "livingly", as they say in Zen, that is, he must obtain the maximum result with the minimum effort and material, and nothing useful must be thrown away. There are stories used to illustrate this theme, and if they are extreme, they point the moral. It is said, for example, that two monks approaching a monastery saw a dead leaf floating down the stream. "Let us go elsewhere," said one of them, "for a Master who allows his pupils to waste but a leaf is no right Master for us!" How different is this close communion with facts and things from the Southern School of Buddhism, which speaks incessantly of the escape from life as the Goal! Zen is not an escape from things but a new way of looking at things, whereby they are seen to be already in Nirvana.

The spirit of Zen is so intoxicating to the newly awakening mind that some form of discipline is needed to offset the dangers of exuberant joy. Humility is taught by precept and practice. Said a Zen Master, "Let one's ideal rise as high as the crown of Vairochana, yet one's life should be so full of humility as to make one prostrate at a baby's feet." "Humility, poverty and inner sanctification—these ideas of Zen are what saves Zen from sinking into the level of the Medieval antinomians. Thus we can see how the Zen-Do discipline plays a great part in the teachings of Zen and their practical application to our daily life."[2] Yet this discipline is largely self-discipline. It is a constant self-recollectedness, a constant awareness, a state of being at all times "mindful and self-

[1] *Gautama the Buddha*, RADHAKRISHNAN, p. 19.
[2] *Essays*, I, p. 316.

possessed". Asked how he exercised himself, a Master replied, "When I am hungry, I eat; when tired, I sleep." The reply was sharp. "That is what everybody does!" "When they eat," said the Master, "they eat, but are thinking of other things, thereby allowing themselves to be disturbed; when they sleep, they do not sleep, but dream of a thousand things." One thing at a time, in full concentration, is the mental discipline.

In the same way the monk is "poor". He is literally poor in possessions, for whatever his wealth at home, in the temple he owns no more than his neighbour, and that, consisting of his robes, a few books, a razor and a set of bowls, will go into the small wooden box which acts as his pillow. More important, however, is the mental element of spiritual poverty, or absence of desire. This has been expressed in a typical Zen way. A pupil asked his Master for the loan of his knife, and the Master handed him his own, blade first. "Please give me the other end," said the pupil. "And what would you be doing with the other end?"

Worldly possessions are not incompatible with the detachment which must in the end precede enlightenment; but they make it much harder. "Money, possessions, honours, ambitions, ready-made formulas, habits, personal interests, how many things hide our own secret value—our Buddha value—from our eyes. For we all possess the same nature as Buddha. What we lack is to be conscious of it, and to favour its complete expansion in ourselves by means of absolute detachment, complete freedom of mind—poverty."[1]

Conjoined to this inward state of spacious poverty, whereby the mind, no longer bound to its own possessions, is free as the clouds and the wind are free, as the light upon the hills at dawn is free, is the delicate virtue of acceptance. It has been brilliantly said that freedom is not in doing what you like but in liking what you do. The next step on the path, be it a theatre, a new job or the washing up, is completely accepted as—the next step on the path, and done as such and not otherwise. Emotion is omitted, and all other types of personal reaction. "For the perfect man employs his mind as a mirror. It grasps nothing: it refuses nothing. It receives, but does not keep. And thus he can triumph over matter without injury to himself."[2] In the light of this it is easy to see what Dr. Suzuki means when he said, "When things are brought to you, just accept them

---

[1] *The Buddhist Sects of Japan*, STEINILBER-OBERLIN, p. 135.
[2] CHUANG TZU, Translated GILES, pp. 97-98.

and say thank you, but do not talk about it. Zen tries to make you accept things, and when you have accepted them you give a hearty laugh."[1] And this laughter is both healing and a symptom of good health. It bubbles up in a thousand stories, creeps into the corners of a thousand famous pictures, and seems to permeate Zen life. Zen is perhaps the only spiritual school in the world which makes deliberate use of laughter in its training, and the Zen life as I knew it is just full of it.

The daily life of the monk may be gathered from several of Dr. Suzuki's books or from *The Pilgrimage of Buddhism* by J. B. Pratt. The purpose of this present volume, however, is rather to make plain how the practice of Zen is not a national affair, nor is it only to be found in a mind whose body lives in a monastery. But wherever the student of Zen may live, his purpose in life is to raise his quality of living, as distinct from his standard of living, his spiritual as distinct from his material wealth. His life will be simple because the complexities of life will have no attraction. He will be poor, for his riches are not to be seen of mortal eye. He will be joyous, for the joy which is the heart of Zen can never be hidden, and like the scent of the rose will travel far upon the sunlit or the midnight air.

The fruits of Zen, then, are the qualities of mind which produce great deeds, great art and culture, and greater still, great men.

[1] From a talk to the Buddhist Society, London, *Buddhism in England,* XI, p. 69.

Chapter 6

But what is Zen?

So far, so good. Or is it? Have we got anywhere at all? Are we a foot nearer Zen, or are we merely learning more and more about it? For Zen is not a new thing but a new way of looking at things. It is a new vision with the old eyes. It is a tardy awakening of the faculty of direct vision, a functioning of habitual consciousness from a plane above and beyond the sway of the opposites.

Being essentially beyond reason, it is useless to reason about it, or to use a normal reasonable approach. One must invent a new technique, and anything is good which serves this end. The ponderous frontal attack of logic and dialectic is here of no avail, and serves but to build up further barriers between the attacker and the attacked (including, be it noted, the notion that there is anything to be attacked or anyone to attack). We must therefore adopt a more fluid plan of campaign, sniping rather than shelling the enemy positions and, in the end, by sheer speed and mobility arriving victorious at the point of our departure. For such is Zen; but let us try again.

Some may find it easier to feel Zen than to think it. Certainly it pertains to the world of poetry and music rather than to that of logic; to the heart and not to the thinking mind. It is, as already described, like a joke. You see it or you don't, for it cannot be explained. The Japanese find it in nature and not in books. Steinilber-Oberlin quotes a Master as saying, "Have you noticed how the pebbles of the road are polished and pure after the rain? True works of art! And the flowers? No word can describe them. One can only murmur an 'Ah!' of admiration. A Japanese writer and bonze has said that one should understand the 'Ah!' of things!"[1]

The "Ah" of things is Zen, for to add anything to this reaction to the beauty of a rose is to spoil the immediacy and therefore the value of the experience.

[1] *The Buddhist Sects of Japan*, p. 133.

For the life of Zen, let us say it once again, is usual life, but usual life with a difference. "The spiritual life," says a Christian mystic, "is not a special career, involving abstraction from the world of things. It is a part of every man's life; and until he has realised it he is not a complete human being, has not entered into possession of all his powers."[1] As Dr. Suzuki said in a talk to the Buddhist Society, London, "When we carry on as we do in our everyday life, there is plenty of Zen in that. But an eye is needed—a third eye. We have two eyes to see two sides of things, but there must be a third eye which will see everything at the same time and yet not see everything. That is to see Zen. Our two eyes see dualistically, and dualism is at the bottom of all trouble. But the third eye is not between or above the two eyes—*the two eyes are the third eye*."

Joshu came to the Master Nansen and asked:

"What is the Tao?"

"Usual life," said Nansen.

"How does one accord with it?"

"If you try to accord with it you will get away from it."

If this does not make sense, or, what is better, illuminating non-sense, bear in mind that the late Sir Walford Davies once said to a choir of working men: "Whatever you do, don't try to sing this tune; just let it sing itself." After all, the humble hiccough arrives by itself, doesn't it?

"Zen lives in facts, fades in abstractions, and is hard to find in our noblest thought." I forget who said that, nor does it matter.

To appreciate its force it is necessary to analyse one's habitual use of consciousness, and to see how minute by minute most of us slide away from facts. We exaggerate them, symbolise them, like them or dislike them, sentimentalise or brutalise them, wrap them up or gloat about them, draw enormous meaning from them or stuff them into the background of the mind, there, if we can, to forget them. Seldom indeed do we accept them gratefully, learn from them, bless them and pass upon our way. The Master Bokuju was asked, "We have to dress and eat every day, and how can we escape from all that?" The Master replied, "We dress, we eat." I don't understand you," said the questioner. "Then put on your dress, and eat your food," said the Master. And then what would he find? That there would be no Zen if he ceased to eat or dress. When hungry we eat; when tired we sleep. Why make a fuss

[1] *Practical Mysticism*, EVELYN UNDERHILL, p. x.

about it, or a poem about it, or a cast-iron habit about it? Why do anything about it save to eat and sleep, or laugh, or love, or live? In the West our minds are filled with the meaning of things, with finding sermons in stones and a collect for the day in everything. Zen is usual life, lived in the consciousness of Zen, that is, in a state of mind in which the tension of the opposites is stilled, having been neither slain nor exorcised, nor denied nor ignored, but—just dropped, or, as one steps over a lowered tennis net when the game is over and not otherwise, transcended. How seldom do we wallow in the moment! Is it not enough when listening to music to pour one's heart and soul into the sound? For now and here, in the scent and colour of the rose, and not in its "meaning", is Zen to be found; in the joy of the moment and not in its cause.

Yet he is a fool who is bound by the facts he uses, and lets another abstract from them a fog in which the flame of Zen will die. As R. H. Blyth has written, "In the life of action we deal only with concrete things, with men and women. But slaves to some definition of it, men die for Freedom, kill themselves for Honour, slaughter millions in the name of Democracy or Communism. Zen denies nothing, has nothing negative in it, but it says, 'Beware of Abstractions!'" Thomas Aquinas was probably right when he said that he who is drawn to something desirable does not desire to have it as a thought but as a thing.

Zen, then, is a way of living life, not a way of escape from it. As Rupert Brooke once said, with sudden passionate vehemence, "There are only three things in the world, one is to read poetry, another is to write poetry, and the best of all is to live poetry!" How true is this of Zen, for what is Zen but a living blend of music, laughter, joy and tears, all lived and loved and known?

All this is futile, and Alan Watts is right. "Anyone who attempts to write about Zen has to encounter unusual difficulties; he can never explain, he can only indicate; he can only go on setting problems and giving hints which at best can bring the reader tantalisingly nearer to the truth, but the moment he attempts any fixed definition the thing slips away. ..."[1] For "that which has been successfully defined has been successfully killed", as someone brightly said. In the end one can only say of Zen, "That's it!"

What's it? Let us try again. This is a steep hill that we have to climb, so let us undress a trifle before we attempt to rush it. Zen *is*, so let us forget that it is anything. Remove philosophy, and with it

[1] *The Spirit of Zen*, p. 12.

theories and classification. Remove religion, and all yearning, for there is nothing for which to yearn. Remove all science, and all learning, for the greatest of Masters stated with pride that he knew nothing of Buddhism—or of Zen. Sit loose to life, the waistcoat buttons undone and the frown erased from the brow; pour out the soiled bath-water of habitual thought, and into the void flows Zen, and with it joy, and a giggle or two of relief, and a new delight in a bottle of beer, or darning, or the morning cup of tea.

For the life of Zen has enormous gusto, which cannot be said for the average professor, scientist or man of God. There is nothing holy about Zen, or "far too technical for the little ones".

> *"Look children,*
> *Hail-stones!*
> *Let's rush out!"*

Thus one of the poems of Basho, the most famous poet of Japan. In England the equivalent poem is in *A Child's Garden of Verses*, not in a book for the "adult" mind.

> *"The friendly cow, all red and white*
> *I love with all my heart;*
> *She gives me cream with all her might*
> *To eat with apple-tart."*

There's enthusiasm for you, for Stevenson had found and lived his Zen. Perhaps you now smile condescendingly, assuming that Zen is for the child at play. So it is, for the child at play, though it has less knowledge, has far more wisdom than its parents, but the power of a child is greater than the oldest adult can control. "Ummon raises his staff. That is all; but it has the power and force of the Niagara Falls, carrying all before it."[1] Joshu says, "Wash your bowls," and these words have more significance than the periods of Burke and Demosthenes. Zen is child-like in the sense that of such are the Kingdom of Heaven, but it is a reveille and not a lullaby, a challenge to the whole of man to become what he is.

Zen is neither here nor there, neither now nor then, yet it is in a special sense extremely and entirely here, and now, and this. It is in all senses im-mediate, without intervention between the fact and its experience. Dwight Goddard puts it well. "Zen has no special forms, nor ritual, nor creeds, unless you call 'Seeing into one's own nature' a creed. They sedulously avoid any slavish adoration of

[1] BLYTH, p. 108.

images, any authority, any priestcraft. But one thing they do believe in and place an exclusive emphasis upon, namely, right concentration of mind. And this, not only in the technical practice of 'Za-Zen', but in their attitude towards everything else, their labour, their begging, their eating, their social contacts. They maintain, throughout the day, an attitude and spirit of 'this one thing I do'."[1] This absolute acceptance of and concentration on the task in hand is part of the method of Zen, whereby the tension in the mind between mediate and im-mediate experience is raised to the point where something has to break. All being well, it is the cast-iron roof of the thought-machine which breaks, and the light and power of the unconscious is allowed to flood the conscious mind.

But let us relax for the moment and shift our point of attack. Consider the essential Buddhist principle of *anicca,* change, so fundamental that it is basic in all the Buddhist Schools of thought. All is flow, a ceaseless flow of life into and out of the forms which, for a time, express some part of it.

Let us consider flow. The river is the obvious analogy. Sit by a river and watch, just watch the flow. There is no hurry but no pause. There are eddies and minor whirlpools on the surface but the flow is constant. It is at once fearful and restful. What fears? The self fears, lest it be swept from its elaborate moorings to possessions, place and circumstance. It fears to flow, to move on, lest it cease to be what it is. Its fears are well-founded, for nothing is ever for two seconds the same, not even self; in fact, psychologists tell us, the self least of all. Why, then, is flow so restful? Because of its sense of becoming, of becoming something more; because of the peace which comes from letting go self-effort; of merging with a process which is coeval with eternity. Evanescence, from the sentimental food of poets, becomes the assurance of eternal life, the knowledge that the self, while it dies every minute, is eternally reborn. For the mind consists in walking and not legs, as someone brightly said, and life only dies when we try to stop its flow. He who takes up a handful of the river does not cease its flow, nor does he hold the river in his hand. The river is its flow, not the water in it which, if it ceased to flow, would cease to be the river. The mind is, therefore, a leaf on the river's flow which, leaping here and there, flows onwards to the sea. That it does not

[1] Zen as a World Religion, *Buddhism in England,* V., p. 114.

know the nature of the sea is immaterial, and the speed of the flow
is relative:

> *"The morning glory blooms but an hour*
> *And yet it differs not at heart*
> *From the giant pine that lives for a thousand years."*

Thus the Japanese poet Matsunaga Teitiku, and a thousand more.

Now the flow is not in the river but in the mind. It follows that
the mind which seeks for Zen must never again sit down. We sit on
the way up the hillside to admire the view, to rest, or to preen
ourselves on the distance we have come. Psychologically, we do
worse than that. We keep sitting down in the belief that we have
arrived, forgetting, in Sir Edwin Arnold's words, that

> *"Veil after veil will lift, but there must be*
> *Veil upon veil behind."*

Until, of course, we realise that there are no veils and nothing for
them to hide. Meanwhile we are always sitting down in the
armchair of a glorious set of words, with smug satisfaction
assuring ourselves that at last we have arrived. Thus many a
student in a Zen class, after a few weeks' puzzled attendance,
announces proudly, "In other words, Zen is"—whatever the box
into which he wants to shut poor Zen away from the sunlight
happens to be called, whether "super-discriminative mysticism" or
"Oriental Quakerism" or some other silly noise in the air. Zen is,
and is not anything. When, therefore, the mind arrives at any stage
of its inner development beware lest it stops, for to stop anywhere
is to stop, and to stop is to die. Life is motion, to live is to flow, and
in thought there should be no such thing as a conclusion. Even an
opinion should be but tentatively held. It is wrong, for it is only
relative, and all that is relative is short of truth itself and therefore
wrong. Get up, then, out of that chair, shake the dust of illusion
from your eyes, and walk on!

Every habit is a limitation of movement, and from this point of
view there are no good habits. How rightly Laurence Binyon
speaks of "the creeping film of habit that clouds the mind". All
habits are blinkers, limiting the field of action or thought or
spiritual sight, and one of our worst habits is to sit in one of the
pairs of opposites and loudly sneer at the other. In *The Religion of
Non-religion*, Friedrich Spiegelberg, speaking of peace and war,
agrees with Graham Howe in *War Dance* that "we cannot live

without our opposites, and granting this fact would be the only guarantee for peace. But he who tries to hold fast to one single idea and not to be changed in his attitude will soon have to fight against the necessity of movement and alteration of every fact. . . . For life means change and going on . . ."[1]

These various ideas are drawn together in Dr. Suzuki's *Buddhism in the Life and Thought of Japan* (p. 27). "The philosophy of intuition takes time at its full value. It permits no ossification, as it were, of each moment. It takes hold of each moment as it is born from Sunyata. Momentariness is therefore characteristic of this philosophy. Each moment is absolute, alive, and significant. The frog leaps, the cricket sings, a dew-drop glitters on the lotus leaf, a breeze passes through the pine branches, and the moonlight falls on the murmuring mountain stream." Compared with this time-philosophy, space-philosophy is like the pile of stone which becomes a vast cathedral compared with the Japanese bamboo, straw-thatched, tea-house which so falls into the scenery that it is hardly seen. The one, however glorious, stands and holds up time; the other flows with it, and being constantly rebuilt may be said to last for ever. The one is a product of a mind which claimed achievement; the other comes from a mind which no more claims achievement than it claims as such the blowing of a nose.

The Master was wishing a friend to enter official employment. He replied, "I am not yet able to rest in the assurance of THIS." The Master was pleased. Thus Confucius, and though at the moment I am not sure of the relevance of the story I like it. But let us pass on.

Where to? The presence of purpose in the mind is a hindrance. It is selective, when North and South and East and West are equally filled with Zen. The Chinese understanding of the Elixir of Life means, according to Jung, "forever tarrying in purposelessness."[2] This is nonsense according to reason, but is it not patently true? Imagine life as an endless field of time and space and a man who rushes, with grim, determined jaw, from one point in it to another. Why *that* point to that *other* point, and why hurry? Which reminds me of the Police Officer in Dublin who, being asked by a stranger the way to a distant part of the city, tried to explain for a while and then, giving it up, declared, "Och, Sir, if I was you I wouldn't *start*

[1] P. 14 of the pamphlet of this name, published by the Buddhist Lodge, London, now the Buddhist Society, London, in 1938.
[2] *The Secret of the Golden Flower*, p. 66.

from here!" That is most excellent Zen, for why this hurry to get from here, which is nowhere in particular, to there, which is nowhere else?

Is Zen still hiding from your worried eyes? It is not hidden. Remember the Master and his disciple in the mountains. The wild laurel was in bloom and the air was redolent. Asked the Zen Master, "Do you smell it?" When his companion nodded, the Master said, "There, I have kept back nothing from you." And if you cannot see your own eyes, or lift yourself up by your belt, you must learn. Zen calls a spade a spade and neither an agricultural implement nor a bloody shovel. Zen says, "I hold a spade and yet I hold it not. Well?" Both are true as neither is true, so what is the answer? Dig.

There is an ancient Chinese saying that in normal consciousness mountains are seen as mountains and trees as trees. But after a while, in the course of one's spiritual journey, mountains no longer appear as mountains, nor trees as trees. But later still, on attaining enlightenment, mountains are once more seen as mountains and trees as trees.

In the beginning mountains are seen as mountains, for so they are to the eye of the senses. There is no tension in the mind between the opposites, least of all between the world of discrimination and the world of non-discrimination. Things are what they seem to be and that is that. Then the mind begins to develop. It begins to think, and the previous sensuous impressions are called into question. Is the mountain really a mountain, or is it a phantasmagoria of the eye? If this sounds foolish, so it is. Only the fool is wise.

Speaking of "immovable intelligence", the ideal virtue of the Japanese fencer, Dr. Suzuki says that it has affinities with Ignorance itself. The beginner in swordsmanship just parries the blow that is aimed at him. He does not think, and does not need to know. Nothing stops his flow of mind and its appropriate action. But as soon as he begins to know, he begins to think, and by the time he has thought what to do his opponent's sword has landed on his head, and neatly cut him in two. But when he knows all there is to know about the art of fencing, he will once more cease to think before acting, and be as "ignorant" as only the fool, the child and the truly spiritual man are satisfied to be. In terms of the mind, "the ignorant have not yet awakened their intelligence and therefore they retain their naïveté. The wise have gone to the end of their intelligence, and therefore they no more resort to it. The two are in a way good neighbours. Only those of 'half knowledge' have their heads filled with discriminations."[1]

Is all about me but a projection from my thought upon the screen of circumstance, having no validity save in the mind which gave it birth? It is all very troubling, for, to use psychological terms, with the birth of the Self and the correspondingly diminished value of the self, a new sense of values appears, and the world is seen with new, though sorely troubled, eyes. All now is stress, though of a different order. A gulf is felt between the old life and the new, between one's former friends and interests and the new way of life which alone gives satisfaction to the ideal-laden mind. In time this inward turmoil leads to the "dark night of the soul" and a sense of loneliness, of severance from the human life about one, which produces an intolerable tension. By the way of analogy, think of a swimmer who enters the sea. First, there is the self and the sea. They are distinct, and though I approach the sea I am of the land and air and move quite freely. Then I enter the water, and immediately the way gets harder. It is more and more difficult to walk; I am pushing a vast and shapeless burden of water in front of me. I am of the land and yet of the sea, and whereas the one no longer helps me the other has not yet fully received me. And so I struggle, buffeted with the waves, pushed here and there, yet still unable to use the sea in which I long to submerge myself. I know the worst of both my worlds and the use of neither.

Then suddenly I swim, and the sea becomes my carrier; it is the world about me and my friend. There is now no effort, no more tension between two differing conditions, no more fear. I am one with the sea and yet am still the self that walked on the firm sea-shore. To phrase the same idea in the form of a Japanese *tanka*,

> *"I look at the sea.*
> *I enter the rival sea.*
> *How hard to walk on!*
> *I give myself to the sea.*
> *Where now is the sea, am I?"*

To return to the previous analogy, mountains are once more mountains and trees are once more trees. Things are no more symbols of something else, but adorably or dirtily or joyfully

---

[1] *Zen Buddhism and its Influence,* pp. 77-78.

themselves. They are accepted for precisely what they are, and then the perceiving mind walks on. Think again of the story of two monks on a journey who came to a ford. What a fearsome burden many of us carry about, of pretty girls, and vain regrets and memories. The girl was a girl and in need of a lift. She had it and the monk walked on.

The Zen way of doing things is to do them. Just like that. I stood at the foot of a high dive, waiting for the courage to climb the steps and dive. I measured the height from the water, worked out how to place my hands and how to fall, considered the temperature of the water, the people in the way and the chances of breaking my neck. All this took time, but I still remained where I was. I had not dived. Finally, I tried the Zen way of diving. I just walked up, took a breath and dived. The same applies to getting up in the morning, writing that letter, or doing those exercises. Just do them before the vast array of emotions can intervene. Now is the best time for everything, because if done now it is im-mediately done, without like or dislike, purpose or desire. For things are what we do with them; they are not good or evil save as we make them so, and the same applies to their being useful, beautiful or just plain dull. Zen lies in how we do things rather than in what we do, and the enlightened man will walk and talk and smoke and laugh quite differently from the man who still thinks politics "matter" and that things are what they seem. The Zen practitioner is in the world and yet not of it; his habitual consciousness is above the opposites, above the discrimination by which we choose just one of a pair of opposites and draw aside our robes from contamination with the other.

Are we becoming philosophical? Let us go straight up the hill. Let us eschew irrelevance and the byways of delightful thought, and go for it. That is where Alice (*Through the Looking-Glass*) describes the Path more accurately than any of the glorious Scriptures of the world. You will remember the beginning of chapter 2: "I should see the garden far better," said Alice to herself, "if I could get to the top of that hill: and here's a path that leads straight to it—at least, no, it doesn't do that—" (after going a few yards along the path, and turning several sharp corners), "but I suppose it will at last. But how curiously it twists! It's more like a corkscrew than a path! Well, *this* turn goes to the hill, I suppose—no, it doesn't! This goes straight back to the house! Well then, I'll try it the other way."

And she did, but it was no use. She tried a dozen ways and, finally, "resolutely turning her back on the house, she set out once more down the path, determined to keep straight on till she got to the hill. For a few minutes all went well, and she was just saying, 'I really *shall* do it this time,' when the path gave a sudden twist and shook itself (as she described it afterwards), and the next moment she found herself actually walking in at the door." This immortal passage is the purest of Zen, while for those who like a ponderous analogy, let the house be the intellect ... or let it be Zen.

But perhaps we are trying too hard. Let us relax again, and let things happen, including the wakening of the flower of Zen. As a patient of Carl Jung wrote to him, "By keeping quiet, repressing nothing, remaining attentive, and hand in hand with that, accepting reality—taking things as they are, and not as I wanted them to be—by doing all this, rare knowledge came to me, and rare powers as well, such as I could never have imagined before. I always thought that when we accept things, they overpower us in one way or another. Now this is not true at all."[1] ... Of course it is not true, and the patient was ill because she thought she was. Things only overwhelm us when we do not accept them. If we just accept them like the weather and a cold in the head and the state of the crops, we shall remain as we are, balanced, integrated and smiling happily. For laughter is the outward sign of an inward state of balance, and a grim face is the sign of a grim condition within. He who has Zen is based upon a rock which the rival seas of the opposites cannot trouble. What is more, he has Zen.

And so for a final smack at the opposites. We begin, as described in Chapter One, with a world in which their sway is all but absolute, and all our actions, motives, thoughts and means of communication are heavily influenced, if not completely dominated, by them. We can try compromise, but all compromise of principle is as weak as compromise in inessentials is wise and advisable. (Remember "Three in the Morning".) But compromise is still on the plane of the opposing forces; we must lift our consciousness to the plane of a "higher third", from which Olympian calm we may look down, with compassion or with a giggle, or just look down, at the battle below. But the higher third is still in the realm of the intellect. Higher than this alone is what is called in the Kegon School of the Mahayana Jijimuge. *Ji* are events, persons, the world of the particular and the concrete. *Ri*

[1] *The Secret of the Golden Flower*, p. 126.

are principles, totalities, the abstractions which lie behind all *Ji*. *Ji* is *rupam*, form, and *Ri* is *sunyata*, the Void. They are the ultimate pair of opposites. Their relation is one of "perfect mutual unimpeded solution". In the same way "Jiji", the manifold items in the world of form, are "Muge". "Each individual *Ji* is not only dissolved unimpededly in *Ri* but also each in the other individually, mutually, and totalistically. So, when I lift a finger, the whole of the world of *Ji* is found dissolved in it, and not only the world as such but each individual reality separately."[1] In other words, as I understand the learned author of that explanation (and I thought I did when I took it down from him), the doorknob is the cat and the cat is the doorknob, but though they are both interfused in one they never cease to be the doorknob and the cat respectively. Which is absurd, but Zen.

So what? Let us consider the technique by which for a thousand years unnumbered Chinese, Korean and Japanese Zen Buddhists have understood this absurdity, and all the other absurdities which are truth in the world beyond the reasoning mind. For the bridge must be made between reason and truth, between conceptual thought and Zen. The process of thought cannot think beyond itself, yet Zen is beyond it. Where is the bridge? The goose is in the bottle. It grows. How to get it out without hurting the goose or breaking the bottle? The answer is clear: "There—it's out!"

[1] *The Essence of Buddhism*, SUZUKI, p. 45.

Chapter 7

Zen Technique

The process of Zen is a leap from thinking to knowing, from second-hand to direct experience. For those unable to make the leap for themselves a bridge must be built which, however rickety, being built for the occasion before being flung away, will land the traveller on the "other shore" of enlightenment. But the best of bridges will still partake of the nature of a leap, of a spark between two terminals, and sense must yield to non-sense before a sense appears compared with which "dull reason's cautious certainty" is dull indeed. But "just as the highest and the lowest notes are equally inaudible, so, perhaps, is the greatest sense and the greatest nonsense equally unintelligible" to the intellect. For, as Alan Watts goes on to say in a well-known passage, "Zen does not attempt to be intelligible, that is, understood by the intellect. The method of Zen is to baffle, excite, puzzle and exhaust the intellect until it is realised that intellection is only thinking *about*; it will provoke, irritate and again exhaust the emotions until it is realised that emotion is only feeling about, and then it contrives, when the disciple has been brought to an intellectual and emotional impasse, to bridge the gap between second-hand, conceptual contact with reality, and first-hand experience."[1]

Any and every type of material may be used in the building of this bridge, yet all of it comes out of the enquirer's mind, for the greatest Master, even the Buddha himself, can only "point the Way". None of the bridge material makes sense. "The masters asked awkward and unanswerable questions; they made fun of logic and metaphysics; they turned orthodox philosophy upside down in order to make it look absurd."[2] The means varied with the questioner, for no two minds which came to the Master were quite the same in their slavery to conceptual thought or in the nature of the chains which bound them. "The Zen master is an adept in the use of a medium which directly points to his Zen experience and by

[1] *The Spirit of Zen*, pp. 11-12.
[2] *Ibid*, 28.

which the questioner, if he is mentally ripe, will at once grasp the master's intention."[1]

Any device would do if it worked. "If I tell you," said the Sixth Patriarch, "that I have a system of Law to transmit to others, I am cheating you. What I do to my disciples is to liberate them from their own bondage with such devices as the case may need."[2]

In Japan, as in China, the most famous devices are the mondo, a form of rapid question and answer which sounds like sparks flashing between two terminals, and the koan, an enigmatic phrase insoluble by the intellect, which is often a compressed form of a mondo. Neither has any meaning for the rational mind. These, however, are but two of the countless "devices" used, and more, no doubt, are being invented.

All presuppose some degree of mental training, for it is obvious that enlightenment in any form implies the mastery of the seeking mind, and mind-control and development are common ground in all the great religions. Asked, "How shall I escape from the wheel of birth and death?" a Master replied, "Who puts you under restraint?" For, as Sir Edwin Arnold wrote in *The Light of Asia*,

> *"Ye suffer from yourselves. None else compels,*
> *None other holds you, that ye live and die,*
> *And whirl upon the wheel, and hug and kiss*
> *Its spokes of agony. ..."*

In the terse phraseology of the *Dhammapada*, "As a fletcher straightens his arrow, so the wise man straightens his unsteady mind, which is so hard to control." Or again, more pithily still, "Irrigators guide water; fletchers straighten arrows; carpenters bend wood; wise men shape themselves."[3] From the earliest days of Indian Yoga, from the Stoics to the present day Theosophists, all who seek enlightenment have agreed on the need of mind-control and subsequent mind-development. "Yoga," says Patan-jali, is "the hindering of the modifications of the thinking principle", and until this "thinking principle" has been brought under control the mind cannot see its object clearly, much less see, as sooner or later it must learn to see, itself. The student of Zen, therefore, learns, like other aspirants for enlightenment, to control his thinking mind, for until he has developed his intellect he cannot

[1] *Philosophy, East and West*, p. 113.
[2] *The Sutra of Wei Lang*, p. 95.
[3] *Dhammapada*, Verses 33 and 145.

rise beyond it. The purpose of all such exercises is, from the first, to "see into one's own nature", and no external force or agency is admitted to exist. "Zen is neither monotheistic nor pantheistic; Zen defies all such designations. Hence there is no object in Zen on which to fix the thought. Zen is a wafting cloud in the sky. No screw fastens it, no string holds it; it moves as it lists. ... Meditation is not Zen."[1]

The moment, therefore, that the student has gained some measure of mental control he begins to destroy the fetters created by his thought. Thereafter meditation becomes a hindrance, not a help. It is "unnatural", in that it hinders the flow of normal life.

A monk sat meditating all day long. His Master asked him what he sought. "My desire is to become a Buddha," said the monk. The Master picked up a piece of brick and began to polish it on a stone. Asked to explain his action, the Master said that he wished to make a mirror. "But no amount of polishing a brick will make it into a mirror," said the monk. "If so, no amount of sitting cross-legged will make thee into a Buddha," said the Master, who for once "explained" his reply. The monk, he said, was trying to attain to Buddhahood. But the Buddha has no fixed forms. "As he has no abiding place anywhere, no-one can take hold of him, nor can he be let go. If thou seekest Buddhahood by thus sitting cross-legged thou murderest him."[2] Thus the element of quietism in meditation, brought from India in the sixth century, was soon expelled by the Chinese Patriarchs. "To meditate," said Wei Lang, "means to realise inwardly the imperturbability of the Essence of Mind"; but "the Essence of Mind is intrinsically pure", and does not need to be purified. All we have to do is to realise that it is pure, and restore our consciousness to where the Essence dwells. "Look within— thou *art* Buddha."[3]

THE STRENUOUS MIDDLE WAY OF ZEN

No mere vacuity of mind will achieve this tremendous result. No "mystical self-intoxication", as Zen has been foolishly called, will reach beyond discrimination, where the opposites are "interfused" in one while remaining two. It is true that all we have to do is to "let go" our desires, our ideals, our conceptual thought, but, as I have

[1] *Introduction to Zen Buddhism*, p. 17.
[2] *Essays* I, p. 222.
[3] *The Voice of the Silence*.

said elsewhere, it needs great courage to let go. In the early stages of his training the student needs tremendous effort and the clearest vision of his immediate goal. As the Master Ummon said to his monks, "If you walk, just walk; if you sit, just sit, but don't *wobble!*" An early stage in mind-development is a foretaste of that "peace of God which passeth all understanding", that serenity of mind which comes from the control of emotion and desire. In the *Message of Bodhidharma*, Dr. Suzuki discusses the meaning of the great man's famous "wall-gazing", which he practised, it is said, for nine years before beginning his mission in China. Far from a negative "contemplation", Dr. Suzuki holds it to mean a keeping of the mind "self-concentrated as a standing cliff, with nothing harassing its imperturbability".[1] This is not negative; far from it, and only those who have achieved satori know the intense, tremendous effort involved in attaining and, paradoxically enough, in holding a state in which

> *"Thought was not; in enjoyment it expired.*
> *No thanks he breathed, he proffered no request;*
> *Rapt in the still communion that transcends*
> *The imperfect offices of prayer and praise."*[2]

The Zen student, as a good Buddhist, treads a Middle Way between effort and letting go, between attachment without and attachment within. "Common people attach themselves to objects without; and within, they fall into the wrong idea of 'vacuity'. When they are able to free themselves from attachment to objects when in contact with objects, and from the fallacious view of annihilation on the doctrine of the 'Void', they will be free from delusions within and illusions without."[3] The wise student goes further. "Let your mind function freely. Whether you are in activity or rest, let your mind abide nowhere—forget the discrimination between a sage and an ordinary man. Ignore the distinction of subject and object. Let the Essence of Mind and all phenomenal objects be in a state of Thusness. Then you will be in Samadhi all the time."

Even upon the foothills of this direct experience, the power of circumstance has been discounted: Death itself, when faced, accepted and, psychologically speaking, "experienced", has no

---

[1] *The Aryan Path*, Vol. 7. p. 10.
[2] From *The Excursion*, Wordsworth.
[3] *Sutra of Wei Lang*, p. 68.

more terrors, and this mental training explains the indifference to death of the Japanese Samurai, whose military training included meditation as well as the physical arts of war. For those who achieve the goal of Zen, meditation has passed beyond the opposites.

> *"For such as, reflecting within themselves,*
> *Testify to the truth of Self-Nature,*
> *To the truth that Self-nature is One-nature,*
> *Have gone beyond the ken of sophistry.*
> *For them opens the gate of the oneness of cause and effect,*
> *And straight runs the path of non-duality and non-trinity.*
> *Abiding with the Not-particular in Particulars,*
> *Whether going or returning they remain unmoved;*
> *Taking hold of the Not-thought in thoughts*
> *In every act they hear the voice of Truth."*[1]

All meditation in Zen is a preparation for this experience, but note that there is no effort to attain, no conscious striving to pass "from the unreal to the Real" or "from darkness to the Light", or any other motion between two opposites. In Zen "there is nothing infinite apart from finite things", nor holy that is not with us here and now. If Zen is not in the room beside you it will not be found in heaven, nor shall any hell withhold it from your eyes. Zen may be wooed in vain in *za-zen*, the formal "sitting" for satori, yet be found in the garden, with a spade in hand. In the same way, the mondo takes place as often in the course of a day's work on the farm as in the silence of the Master's room, and the rising spiritual excitement, as I call it, which often heralds a moment of satori, may come when washing up, or shaving, no less than in the meditation hour.

If this chapter has come some way before the typical Zen "devices" are described, it is because I have noticed a western tendency to confuse and identify Zen with the koan and the mondo, and even with occasional violence used by a Master to help his disciple break through the bars of his own conceptual thought. Yet none is essential to Zen and Zen is none of them. They are, however, still used in Japan and form a large part of the literature of Zen as it comes to us from its Chinese and Japanese past.

---

[1] From the famous *Song of Meditation* of the Zen Master, Hakuin. There are many translations. This is from DR. SUZUKI'S version in an article on "The Meditation Hall and the Monkish Life". (*The Eastern Buddhist,* Vol. 2, p. 49.)

When Bodhidharma "came from the West" to China in the sixth century A.D. he was regarded as something of a heretic, for his abrupt and im-mediate style of teaching was far removed from the philosophical enquiry of his fellow Indian Buddhists. When, therefore, in the succeeding centuries, monasteries were formed about some Master, much of the Indian Buddhist technique was still observed. It was not for a century or two after the re-founding of the School of Zen by Yeno (Hui-neng) that the koan and mondo became, as it were, a system of teaching, and those recorded up to that time were preserved as historical notes rather than as present means of enlightenment. Their adoption, however, as a working technique for attaining satori, changed the face of the movement, and gave it the dynamic quality which to this day preserves it as one of the formative forces in Japan. Historically, therefore, the importance of the koan and mondo is difficult to over-estimate. Dr. Suzuki says "the koan system has effected a special development in Zen Buddhism, and is a unique contribution which Zen has made to the history of religious consciousness. When the importance of the koan is understood, we may say that more than the half of Zen is understood."[1]

The nature of a koan is best explained by a few examples. "Is there Buddha-nature in a dog?" asked a monk. "Mu" (No) said the Master, and Mu is the most famous of all koans. Another is "When your mind is not dwelling on good or evil, what is your original face before you were born?", and this "original face" is now a technical term in Zen Buddhism. A third famous koan is "the sound of one hand clapping". Two hands clapped make a well-known sound. What is the sound of one? Here are others: "What was the reason of Bodhidharma's coming from the West?" "If all things are reducible to the One, to what is the One to be reduced?" "Who is he with no companion among the 'ten thousand things' (phenomena)?" The goose in the bottle, already used in these pages, is another famous koan, and here is another problem insoluble by the intellect. A man hangs over a precipice by his teeth, which are clenched in the branch of a tree. His hands are full and his feet cannot reach the face of the precipice. A friend then asks him, "What is Zen?" What answer would *you* make if you were he?

All these are insoluble, and not meant to be intellectually "solved". They are mental cathartics, having an explosive effect in

[1] *Essays* II, p. 3.

THE SOUND of ONE HAND

THE FAMOUS KOAN, "THE SOUND OF ONE HAND CLAPPING"

A woodcut by Hasuko (Mrs. Christmas Humphreys)

the mind which is more than uncomfortable. Indeed, Dr. Suzuki likens them to "deadly poisons which, when taken, cause such a violent pain as to make one's intestines wriggle nine times and more, as the Chinese would say".[1]

Preparation is therefore needed before they can be safely used, and the following is given as the minimum mental equipment. To awaken a sincere desire to be delivered from the bondage of Karma (cause-effect); to recognise that the aim of the Buddhist life is to attain enlightenment; to realise the futility of all intellectual efforts to reach this aim; to believe that the realisation of satori means the awakening of Buddhata (the Buddhist principle within); and finally to be in possession of a strong "spirit of enquiry", which is essential to the attainment of satori.[2]

These preparations made, the first koan is dropped into the mind as a stone into a pool. Then the fun begins. The Master's purpose in supplying the koan is to reproduce in the mind of the pupil the state of consciousness of which the koan is the expression. "That is to say, when the koans are understood, the Master's state of mind is understood, which is satori, and without which Zen is a sealed book."[3]

The technique is to produce a cul-de-sac in the thinking mind, to close all avenues whereby a meaning may be extracted from the given phrase, and to work up the psychic tension until the only way out of the cul-de-sac is to burst the walls which make it. This sounds unpleasant and it is. The expressions used to denote the experience, "the bursting of the bag", "the breaking up of the void", all speak of a moment of sudden and vast release of tension. The sweat pours off the triumphant student, and he cries aloud with joy, for the barriers of a full life's making or, as the Buddhist would say, of many a long life's making have been swept aside. "Broken the ridge-pole of this house of pain," and the self is free because the self is dead.

All this, however, is the culmination of a long period of preparation, either in this life or in previous lives. The whole of the man is bent to the task in hand. The whole powers of the intellect are brought to bear on the problem, not merely for a daily period of time but for every moment of the waking day and probably in sleep. Oblivious to all else, the student wrestles fiercely with his

[1] *Essays* I, p. 18.
[2] *Essays* II, p. 98.
[3] *Essays* II, p. 69.

THE FAMOUS KOAN, "DROP IT"

A drawing by Hasuko (Mrs. Christmas Humphreys)

enemy. Eating, working, doing his temple "chores", no less than in
the long hours of his "still communion", the coldly directed will of
the aspirant struggles to be free. Again and again he returns to his
Master, who, watching him with an old, experienced eye, gives
such experienced help as his wisdom may direct, but never allows
the fighter's tremendous tension to relax. While the mind still
seeks some intellectual escape there is the slight relief of lateral
movement; not till the mental extremity admits no rational escape
does the real battle begin. Now the tiger is trapped and struggles
violently to be free. The tension rises; often the body breaks under
the strain and the man is ill. He may refuse all food, be feverish,
unsleeping, wild in his regard. He cares not, and the Master
watches him. Why live, if to live be a life of slavery? To pass
beyond the discriminative world of false antitheses, to KNOW that
all is One, here's glory worth the winning, and at the end of it to
KNOW that the two that are one are also two, that still the sun will
rise and set, and still the morning blossom with the rose.

All this pertains to the realm of psychology, and a psychological
approach to the koan is probably the best for the western mind.
Dr. Suzuki, himself a student of Carl Jung, has attempted this
approach. The purpose of the koan, he says, is "to bring about a
highly wrought-up state of consciousness. The reasoning faculty is
kept in abeyance, that is, the more superficial activity of the mind
is set at rest so that its more central and profound parts can be
brought out and exercised to perform their native functions."
Meanwhile, he goes on, "the affective and conative centres are
charged to do their utmost in the solution of the koan." This is
what the Zen Master means when he refers to "great faith", and
"great spirit of enquiry", for the faith is a faith in the certainty of
success and the spirit of enquiry is the will to achieve it. "When the
mental integration reaches its highest mark, there obtains a
neutral state of consciousness which is not to be confused with the
'ecstasy' of students of religious consciousness." For the latter is a
static "contemplation" of Reality, while satori, when achieved,
attains poetic relationship with the Unconscious. Finally, the
mind becomes charged with energies hitherto undreamed of. "A
penetrating insight is born of the inner depths of consciousness, as
the source of a new life has been tapped."[1]

But Carl Jung himself has turned his attention to the koan, and
when one of the greatest minds in the West is focused on the

[1] *Essays* II, p. 84.

supreme enigma of the East, something of interest is born. In his Foreword to Dr. Suzuki's *Introduction to Zen Buddhism* (as translated for the Collected Works edition by Constance Rolfe) he approaches Zen, if I may disrespectfully say so, like a cat approaching a hedgehog, prepared at least to disapprove and if need be to retire, though saving face by asserting that such things, though possibly useful in their place, should not be encouraged in a western garden. He appreciates at once, however, that satori is in fact "a matter of natural occurrence, so simple, that one fails to see the wood for the trees, and in attempting to explain it one invariably says the very thing that drives the hearer's mind into a worse confusion". How right he is: Zen vision, he fully appreciates, is not that something different is seen, but that one sees differently; hence the impossibility of describing such a purely subjective experience. To him the fascination of Zen seems to be its lack of supposition, that is, of pre-dispositions of thought or belief. The Buddhist assumes nothing, neither a First Cause nor a Personal God nor a "soul", but the koan is designed to empty the mind of the suppositions or thought-deposits which clog the machinery of flow. For it is one thing to agree intellectually that one should have no suppositions; quite another to keep the mind so fluid that none form. Nothing, no-thing, no single thing, not even beautiful abstractions like Duty, Honour, or Playing the Game, must remain in the mind when Zen is born. For these are but forms of life, whether "good", "bad", or "indifferent", and Zen is beyond *all* forms. When Zen is allowed to flood the mind to the exclusion of all else, these earlier loves may return, for never again will they stand between the observer and the sun. For the koan, or some other means of im-mediate awareness, will have wrought such a transformation in the mind that the various modes of perceiving consciousness, whether labelled the "self" or "id" or "ego" or "soul", will have fallen into place and produced, from a chaos of opposing forces, an ordered plan.

This, however, is but half the battle. There is still unconscious supposition, "the unperceived psychological predisposition" which equates to some degree with the *sankhâras* of Pali Buddhism. "What the unconscious nature of the student opposes to the teacher or to the koan as an answer is manifestly satori," which is the "seeing into one's own nature" of the teaching ascribed to Bodhidharma. Now the unconscious "the unglimpsable completeness" of the man, "the matrix of all metaphysical assertions, of all mythology, of all philosophy (in so far as it is not merely critical) and all forms of life which are based upon psychological suppositions", is not merely the "dark" half of the man; it is to the total man as the ocean to the drop, and the purpose and result of the koan technique is to break down the barriers which define the illusory self, and to let in the flood-tide of the universe. On the border, as it were, of the conscious and unconscious circles of the mind is born the Self which grows in proportion as the false self, the *"anatta"* self, dies down, as a fire dies down for want of fuelling. The disintegration of this illusory self, however, before the true Self, which progressively integrates the total man, is born, is filled with danger, and there must be a well-developed and reasonably stable mind on which the experiment of hastening nature may be safely made. Hence the need of a teacher to assist at the death of the false self and the birth of the true, for if the tension created in the mind for the Magnum Opus is wrongly directed, or held too long without the relief of satori, it may wreck the instrument.

All this, however, is only my own understanding of the koan technique and of Dr. Jung's remarks upon it, and the genuine student should study the two great minds for himself. The Essay entitled the Koan Exercise in Dr. Suzuki's *Essays in Zen Buddhism*, Vol. II, will give the Zen technique; the Foreword already quoted will give Dr. Jung's "reply".

There are said to be at least 1,700 koans, but, as Dr. Suzuki says, "for all practical purposes, less than ten, or even less than five, or just one may be sufficient to open one's mind to the ultimate truth of Zen. . . . Only let one gain an all-viewing and entirely satisfying insight into the living actuality of things and the koans will take care of themselves."[1] It has been said that the koan is chosen by the Master to produce a particular result, but of this I know nothing. I do know, however, that a koan may come out of a Zen experience. Thus, "the hill goes up and down" was produced from what I believe to have been a Zen "experience", and the same applies, though it has an intellectual meaning, to my own description of Zen pantheism: "All is God, and there is no God."

The mondo is a rapid question and answer, some of which are together used as a koan for other students. The language used is in one sense mystical to a degree, for it makes no sense to the reason. Nor is the question asked for information. The questioner "leads

[1] *Introduction to Zen Buddhism*, p. 128.

out" his mind, so to speak, to show its insufficiencies, and the Master sees thereby where the student has stuck on the sandbank of a still remaining thought. By his answer, rapidly given, he attempts to blow up the obstruction, as an expert frees the jammed up logs in the river, and allows them to flow once more to the sea. There is here no argument, and generally no explanation. The pupil "sees" or he does not see. If he sees, the Master may give him a further koan; if not, he makes the new answer his koan until that at least is "solved"! As the answer is personal to the pupil, it matters not that a dozen different answers may be given to the self-same question on the self-same day. Thousands of anxious students have asked why Bodhidharma came from the West, and who is the Buddha. Thousands have enquired as to the nature of Zen.

The answers have, of course, been classified, for of such is the human mind, though not the Kingdom of Zen. As early as the tenth century a Zen disciple made a list of eighteen types of question.[1] They range from the question asked to clarify the pupil's mind to that which frankly tested the Master's own ability. Thus a pupil: "How is it that one who understands not, never cherishes a doubt?" Replied the Master, "When a tortoise walks on the ground, he cannot help leaving traces in the mud," which ought to have satisfied the doubts of that young man. But all the types have this in common, that the answer lies in the questioner's mind, and in the intuitive part of it. Always the attack is turned back on the attacker; always the avenues of escape are closed. "All things are such as they are from the beginning; what is that which is beyond existence?" The answer comes like a blow in the face, "Your statement is quite plain; what is the use of asking me?" This is not impatience, or impertinence. It is saying, but with far more force than saying it rationally ... well, surely it is obvious what it is saying.

Dr. Suzuki has attempted his own classification. His main division is into the Verbal and Direct Methods of demonstrating the truths of Zen, the former, or mondo, being subdivided into Paradox, Going beyond Opposites, Contradiction, Affirmation, Repetition and Exclamation. Examples of all will be found in the pages of his manifold writing on Zen. If it is right that "those who have realised the Essence of Mind give suitable answers according to the temperament of the enquirer",[2] such variety must be

[1] *Essays* II, p. 62.
[2] *Sutra of Wei Lang*, p. 96.

expected. Nor is the answer which is given to any one man to be regarded, still less handed down, as in itself a definite teaching. Huang Po makes this perfectly clear.[1] "It is wrong to pick on a certain teaching as suitable to a particular occasion, and preserve it in writing to serve as an unshakeable deduction. Why so? Because in actual fact there is no unalterable Dharma which the Tathâgata (the Buddha) could have preached. ..."

Not all the mondo are confined to one question and its "reply". Some are a rapid fire of question-answer like a fencing-match of words, in which the pupil strives (for his own enlightenment) to pierce the smooth and smiling armour of the Master's serenity, and the Master parries and strikes back, as the pupil's efforts to free himself require.

"What is the one word?"
"What do you say?"
"What is the one word?"
"You make it two."

Sometimes another Master, of the same period or many hundreds of years later, will comment on a previous master's mondo. These comments are known as *nenro*, which means "playful criticism", but to the enlightened or about to be enlightened mind they add to the original mondo. Thus, a monk asked Joshu for instruction in Zen. "Have you had your breakfast or not?" "Yes, Master." "If so, have your dishes washed," was the reply, and the questioner's eye was opened. Ummon, who lived some fifty years later, made a typically Zen comment on this answer. "Was there any special instruction in the remark of Joshu, or not? If there was, what was it? If there was not, what satori was it that the monk attained?" Fifty years later a third Master, Umpo Monyetsu, remarked of the comment of Ummon, "The great master Ummon does not know what is what; hence this comment of his. It was altogether unnecessary; it was like painting legs to the snake and growing a beard to the eunuch. My view differs from his: that monk who seems to have attained satori goes straight to hell!"[2]

This is not flippancy, and the humour is part of the method of Zen. These comments are meant for the hearer's profound consideration, as of koan value. Note that the succeeding

[1] *The Huang Po Doctrine of Universal Mind*, pp. 43-44.
[2] *Essays* I, p. 224.

commentators make things in no way easier. As Dr. Suzuki says, "the Zen master's advice is like pouring oil on a fire; instead of being an escape in the ordinary sense of the word, it is aggravating pain, bringing it to its acutest point."[1]

For the whole of his working day the student keeps his mind in a condition of poised attentiveness, a balanced mean between aggressive strain and placid passivity. On the one hand there is an intense "spirit of enquiry", a powerful unceasing pressure of the will to its objective, to break that koan, to smash the barriers of thought, to KNOW. On the other hand there is the quiet relaxed 'inaction' known to the mystics of all ages. This utter yielding of all effort, all positive will to achievement, is an abandonment of self which amounts to an emptying of the mind of all positive content. Christian mysticism is full of this technique, as James' *Varieties of Religious Experience* and many a later book make plain. Nor is it a western prerogative. As the Taoist, Chuang Tzu, wrote, "The perfect man employs his mind as a mirror. It grasps nothing; it refuses nothing. It receives, but does not keep." When the mind is empty of (the unreal) self, Tao or Zen or the Light or Life, or whatever one cares to call what Bucke called Cosmic Consciousness, pours in. But there are dangers in passivity, as in all extremes. Zen treads the Middle Way, holding the mind one-pointed, lifted with "the whole soul's will", yet open, receptive, eager to welcome the satori for which by negative means it strives, and by striving it achieves passivity.

The koan and mondo are the principle "devices" used by Zen Masters to assist a pupil to cleanse his mind of the fetters of thought, the former being unique in the whole range of religious literature. The mondo, however, is only one of a dozen ways in which the Master, face to face with the pupil, tries to help him. In all these methods the pupil "leads" his mind, so to speak, and awaits the Master's reply. He may ask a question or he may do something, and the Master's reply may be an oral answer, or action, or silence. In any event it will be appropriate to the questioner's state of mind, and be highly charged with (Zen) meaning. The pupil may approach the Master at any hour of the day, in addition to the formal interviews or *san-zen* in the Master's room. He may "open" his mind by a gesture. He may shut the door in the Master's face, knock his spade out of his hand, put something in front of him or take it away. The Master may answer

Buddhism in the Life and Thought of Japan, p. 6.

in words, or with a gesture, or with unpleasant and not in the least playful blows. These occasions, when preserved, are handed down as *innen*, "incidents", and are often more illuminating to the western mind than the mondo.

Huang Po (Jap: Obaku, founder of the third school of Zen Buddhism) was paying reverence to the Buddha image in the temple shrine. A pupil approached and said, "If we ought not to seek Zen through the Buddha, nor through the Dharma (the Doctrine) nor through the Sangha (the monastic Order), why do you bow to the Buddha as if wishing to get something by this pious act?" "I do not seek it," answered the Master, "through the Buddha, nor through the Dharma, nor through the Sangha. I just go on with this act of piety to the Buddha." The pupil asked, "But what is the use of looking so sanctimonious?" The Master gave him a slap in the face, at which he complained, "How rude you are!" "Do you know where you are?" replied the Master. "In this place (in the shrine) I have no time to consider for your sake what rudeness or politeness means." And another slap was given.[1] Do you "see"?

Or again. When Hyakujo was with his Master, a flock of geese flew overhead. "What are they?" asked the Master, himself giving the "lead" for once. "They are wild geese, sir." "Whither are they flying?" "They have flown away, sir." Baso fiercely tweaked his nose, and said, "You say they have flown away, but all the same they have been here from the very beginning." Hyakujo's back was wet with perspiration. He had satori.[2]

This latter is a good example of the "centre-returning" method of the Master's reply. The pupil's mind has a tendency to flow away to the edge of the circle, to escape from "this", and "now". The Master brings it back, and the pupil ultimately "sees". Here is another "incident". The famous Tokusan was sitting outside his Master's house on the verandah, striving to accomplish Zen. His Master asked from within, "Why don't you come in?" "It is dark," said Tokusan. A candle was lighted and handed to him, but as he was about to take it, the Master blew it out. Tokusan was enlightened.

Sometimes the Master forced the issue with a class of pupils. A Master held out a stick (*shippe*) to his audience and said, "Call it not a stick; if you do, you assert. Nor deny that it is a stick; if you

[1] *Introduction to Zen Buddhism*, p. 35.
[2] *Essays* I, p. 225.

do, you negate. Without affirmation or denial, speak, speak!" This sudden demand to do something, anything which would burst the tyranny of the opposites, is typical of Zen. Sometimes the Master had a favourite trick, like Rinzai's shout of "Kwats", which he roared at his thought-entangled followers. And *everything* had to be emptied from the mind before the Master was satisfied. When a pupil asked his Master, "Zen emphasises the need of the expulsion of every idea. Am I right when I have no idea?" the Master replied, "Throw away that idea of yours." "I have told you that I have no idea. What can I throw away?" Said the Master, "You are free, of course, to carry about with you that useless idea of no idea!"

The Master's method was always concrete; the vague abstraction has no place in Zen. Someone asked a Master, "Summer comes, winter comes. How shall we escape from it?" "Why not go where there is neither winter nor summer?" asked the Master. "And where is that?" "When winter comes you shiver," said the Master; "when summer comes you perspire."

Even the Buddhist doctrine of the "great compassionate heart", the power of Maha-Karuna, which, with Maha-Prajna, "great wisdom", is one of the two pillars on which the Mahayana rests, is taught concretely. One day an officer-disciple was late in arriving at his Master's house. He apologised and said that he had been watching a polo match. "Were the men tired?" asked the Master. "Yes, Master." "Were the horses tired?" "Yes, Master." "Is the wooden post here tired too?" The pupil failed to answer. That night he could not sleep, but at dawn hurried back to the Master. The answer had come to him. He asked the Master to repeat the question, which he did. "Yes, Master," he said, and the Master was delighted. A later Roshi pointed out that unless the post was tired there could be no tiredness anywhere.[1]

Often a silent gesture by Master or pupil reveals the content of the mind. A Master wanted a pupil capable of founding a branch monastery elsewhere. The most amazing tests were applied to the various applicants. Finally a monk was chosen as soon as he walked into the room. The head monk, overlooked, was furious, and a contest was prepared. When all the monks were assembled, the Master produced a pitcher. "Do not call this a pitcher," he said. "What *would* you call it?" One said, "You could not call it a block of wood." The Master was not satisfied, and beckoned the monk

---

[1] *The Essence of Buddhism.* p. 54.

he had chosen to come forward. The latter gently pushed over the pitcher, and left the room. He won.

For silence in the end is the only medium for a truth which lies beyond words. "The Tao that can be expressed is not the eternal Tao." The silence to some questions is indeed "deafening like thunder". For the silence of a Master is dynamic, healing, filled with grace. The man as he is, as his enlightenment has made him, speaks to the man who has not yet found himself. "When you speak so loudly I cannot hear what you say," said Emerson, who refused to let himself be distracted by words "about" the subject, when he had the direct experience. "He who knows does not speak. He who speaks does not know," said Lao-Tze. Yet, as Edmond Holmes has pointed out, there are times when "the perception itself imperatively demands expression in order that, in and through the struggle of the artistic consciousness to do full justice to it, it may gradually realise its hidden potentialities, discover its inner meaning and find its true self".[1] This is the birth of art, and the urge of the Master to teach what he knows in order that thereby the knowledge may be "stamped" within him.

For the transmission of Zen knowledge has its own technique. No ordinary Scripture or collection of sermons will here avail. Nor will the record of strange mondo, innen or "incidents" suffice. For the releasing word or gesture of the Master has no transferable significance. If in answer to the question, "What is the Buddha?" a Master answers "three pounds of flax", or "a dirt-scraper" or even a torn umbrella, the reply does not in itself release a later student's mind. A Master is far more than a man who has found satori. After the Zen experience the would-be master goes through a long period of "maturing". "The monk's life, in and out, must grow in perfect unison with this attainment. To do this a further period of training is necessary. His intellectual attainments must be further put to trial by coming in actual contact with the world."[2] There are no rules for this maturing. The individual may retire to the mountains or live in the market place, but in the end he is so soaked in Zen, as it were, that all his reactions will come from a point beyond the intellect. Thereafter he may return to the monastic life and be accepted as a Roshi, prepared to face the tremendous strain of a hundred minds or more attacking his own

[1] Quoted in CRANMER-BYNG'S *Vision of Asia*, p. 237.
[2] *The Eastern Buddhist*, Vol. II, pp. 53-54.

at all hours of the waking day with a view to arriving at the same thought-cleansed enlightenment.

As is fully set out in a number of Dr. Suzuki's works, the life of the Zen monk differs from that of his western equivalent in that there are no "holy offices", nor any time when the mind is at rest from the task of self-enlightenment. There is neither work nor play. All is subordinate to the task in hand, the attainment of satori. But though the koan is held in the mind by night and day, and the Master is available wherever he may be, there is the formal life of the Zen-Do, the Meditation Hall, with long hours of "meditation", in the sense of full concentration on the koan in hand. At these times the Master is always available in his room for *san-zen,* a somewhat terrifying interview. For as soon as the formal bows are made, all ceremony is cast aside. The monk attacks the Master's mind and the Master "replies" with the same tremendous concentration of energy, "What do you say when I come to you with nothing?" "Fling it down." "I said I had nothing. What shall I let go?" "If so, take it away." There is no "sense" in these conversations, yet the purpose is crystal-clear, to grasp a Truth beyond the limited, second-hand, built-up versions of truth that men call sense.

Not only the monk who, for a time, has given his life to Zen may have this Zen instruction. Laymen, accepted for teaching by the Roshi, may come for a period, and often give up their annual holiday for such a period of intensive training. They may attend the super-intensive periods of *sesshin*, which generally last a week per month during a summer and winter season. The strain on the Master must be enormous, for all inessential work in the fields is given up, and for hour after hour the whole of the monastery is locked in full meditation, with a queue of anxious, hopeful or even triumphant monks waiting their turn for the Roshi to confirm, reject or make further suggestions for their inward labours. At other times, as already explained, the Zen experience may come in the fields or in the kitchen, and the stories told herein have shown the remarkable ways by which that experience is achieved.

As a final word in a very long chapter, let me attempt to answer a question often asked. I asked it myself on the first occasion that I rose in a snow-filled darkness and, after an hour's meditation in the Zen-Do, followed the file of monks to the Hon-Do or main hall of the monastery which contains the Buddha-shrine. The altar was gorgeous, the richness of the chaste and perfectly appointed hangings, vestments and altar furnishings being immensely pleasing to the eye. The air was filled with incense and the sound of chanting, and the Master of the monastery moved to and fro with powerful dignity. But what on earth, I asked myself, as I sat at the side and watched it all, has this to do with Zen? The answer, I think, is psychological. The collective formality of these services, while cleansing the mind for the day's work on Zen, provides an effective contrast to the intensely individual and informal nature of Zen technique. The very binding of the mind so tightly gives it the impetus to be free, and if this is of use in any country it is doubly so in Japan, where the formal life of the family and the power of tradition is a factor which cannot be ignored. There is no congregation at that hour of the day, and although in the afternoon service there is often a handful of public to listen to a sermon attuned to the popular need, there is no idea in Zen of a sacrament for the commonweal, for in the absence of a God to save or a soul to be saved how could there be? Meanwhile, the service over, the individual monk, by the use of this device or that, turns the whole strength of his will on the solving of that which cannot be solved, on the understanding of that which lies beyond understanding, in the pursuit of a truth that can never be found, for when was it lost?

Chapter 8

Satori

There can be no Zen without satori. For Zen *is* satori, and all the talk about Zen is only about it. As a Master said: "Satori is the measure of Zen," and it is, of course, the measure of Buddhism. For Buddhism springs from the Buddha's satori, or Enlightenment, and has no meaning without it. The *koan*, the *mondo*, the *innen* or "incidents", all these are incidental to Zen and unnecessary to it. But satori is the goal, the meaning and the heart of Zen. We live in a world of discrimination; satori is the world of non-discrimination, non-differentiation, of two-ness become one-ness and yet equally seen as two. Satori is the world of perpetual now and here and this, of absolute, unimpeded flow. How, then, to build a bridge between these two apparently opposing worlds?

The intellect will go so far and no further. We may learn more and more about Zen; we may pile up simile, analogy and story mountains-high, but still we are only learning "about it and about". We are not experiencing Zen. I touch or see or taste; I feel, whether joy or fear; I KNOW by the intuition—this is experience. I know that I feel, I say that I know, I think that I hear—all this is mediate, second-hand experience. I hold up a finger; this is Zen. I say that I hold up a finger; the Zen has fled. How to keep hold of this living, flowing, im-mediate experience, this sense of perpetual Now?

The means are as many as the efforts of men. The koan and the mondo are two of them, but scores have attained satori who have never heard of either. Any device is good which works, and a thousand more have yet to be found and used as men have need of them. All, however, will have in common the emptying of the self, that into the space so made the light of life, the eternal More, may flow. Everything must be emptied out, the toys that we love, each cherished, loved ideal as well as each "fond offence", all purpose and desire. The self, with its pride and regret of the past, its fears and boasts and desires of the moment, its hopes and ambitions for the days unborn, must be transcended.

Even the approach to the bridge involves enormous effort. "Knock and it shall be opened unto you" is true. It is also true that "our whole existence must be thrown down at the door"[1] or, as I would have put it, thrown *at* the door. The preparation is usually long, but depends, of course, on the individual. And as the man is his mind, and the mind is the net resultant of its own past causes, created in this life and in scores of lives gone by, the variety of mind which seeks for satori is all but infinite. The effort required is therefore equally various, having this in common, that "You yourself must make the effort. (Even) Buddhas do but point the way".[2] The preparation, as already said, may be made in the monastery or in the world of men. "When occupations come to us we must accept them, when things come to us we must understand them from the ground up. If the occupations are regulated by correct thoughts the Light is not scattered by outside things, but circulates according to its own law."[3] Indeed the preparations include the acceptance of all limitations of Karma, for to refuse to accept them, or anything whatsoever, is to perpetuate the division between this and that of which satori is the end. Yet even the attempt to acquire satori must at the final moment be cast away. "The Tao," says Alan Watts, "is not brought to birth by deep philosophical understanding or by any effort of action or emotion, although it is necessary and inevitable that one of these attempts should precede the birth. The birth itself, however, only takes place when the futility of the attempt has been fully realised, and that realisation can only come through making the attempt."[4] But this is only another of the countless paradoxes which, like a hedgehog's prickles, stand erect at the entrance to satori. Another is that with the approach to satori the mind is enormously expanded and contracted at the same time. "Each single fact of experience is to be related to the totality of things, for thereby it gains for the first time its meaning." The part *is* the whole, and the whole of it, and if that is not difficult enough to understand, be pleased to notice that the part is greater than the whole. For the whole is complete, which is finite; the part is unfinished, and that is infinite. ... But at the same time the mind is enormously lessened in content, being contracted to the needle point of this and here

---

[1] *Living by Zen*, p. 125.
[2] *Dhammapada*, v, 276.
[3] *The Secret of the Golden Flower*, p. 57.
[4] *The Legacy of Asia and Western Man*, p. 106.

and now. Philosophers speak of a lessening of the not-Self till the self is all, and of a growing of the Self till the self is squeezed out of existence. Zen does both at once.... And the oil in the machine for this fearful effort? Laughter, and lots of it. Humour is sanity, a release of interior tension with a sudden vision of the fun of things.

The binding power of words and concepts must in the end be severed; we must learn to use them and let them go. For "what distinguishes Zen conspicuously from other spiritual teachings is its assuming perfect mastery over words and concepts. Instead of becoming a slave to them, it is aware of the role they play in human experience, and assigns them to the place to which they properly belong".[1] A monk asked a Master, "Show me the way without appealing to words." Said the Master, "Ask me without using words."

As the shrine of satori is approached, words fall away to silence, or sudden laughter, or a biff on the jaw. Yet, curiously enough, the average student begins by asking questions, and when he realises that none worth asking can in fact be "answered", he falls too soon to silence. It is then that the Master, seeing his audience tied, as it were, in the knots of the opposites, forces the issue. "Speak", he cries, "speak! Speak!" Yet this is a special "speaking". The Master wants a sign, any sign, that the student is freed from the opposites, not tied to them. Isan sent the Master Kyozen a mirror. Kyozen held it before his monks and said, "Is this Isan's mirror or my own? If you say that it is Isan's, how is it in my hands? If you say it is mine, has it not come from Isan? Speak, speak! If not, it will be smashed to pieces." None of the audience showed in some way or another that he could pass between these opposites, and the mirror was smashed.

Nor is the approach to Zen, which (as Alice found when she went through the Looking-Glass) is about as straight as a corkscrew, even onward, much less straight on. It is, indeed, a retreat from bifurcation or the division of unity into the opposites. Instead of healing duality, it retreats to a state of mind— presumably the pre-conscious of western psychology—before the oneness was split by the intellect in two. As Aldous Huxley says: "To those who seek first the Kingdom of God all the rest will be added. For those who, like the modern idolators of progress, seek first all the rest in the expectation that (after the harnessing of atomic power and the next revolution but three) the Kingdom of

God will be added, everything will be taken away. ... 'Our Kingdom go' is the necessary and unavoidable corollary of 'Thy Kingdom come'."[1] And with the Kingdom of Mammon with its "gin, jazz and politics" sense of values, all "vulgar thoughts" must go, not only those which, until recently, were not expressed in the drawing-room, but all thoughts and imaginings that are based on dualism.

"Seek ye first the Kingdom of Heaven." To achieve this end, the koan is the most famous Zen "device". "The Zen master has by his satori attained a vantage ground from which he sallies out to attack the opponent's camp in any direction. The vantage ground is not located at any definite point in space, and cannot be assailed by concepts or any system based on them. The psychologist, philosopher or theologian of any hue falls short of catching him out at his work, for as he does not mind contradicting himself he is out of bounds to any rational argument."[2] The Master, having broken the limits of conceptual space and time, is ever at the centre of a circle whose centre is nowhere and its circumference everywhere. From such a centre he rushes out to deal with events as the spider on its famous web. "Stating this psychologically, anything that happens at the periphery of human consciousness sends its vibration down to the Zen centre of unconsciousness." This produces, in those in whom the intuition has begun to function, a "Zen sense" which will lead, as a candle in the darkness, to the feet of a Master who will guide the student's energies into the cul-de-sac of the intellect, and drive him up to the end. Whatever the poor monk does with his koan will be wrong. He will be abused, ignored, sneered at, struck, but he will never give up. If he does, he will not reach satori; if he fights till he drops he will, as he rolls on the floor, achieve it. Then, in the fierce intensity of the mondo, his mind will be sharpened and sharpened until by a process of ultra rapid reasoning he transcends all reasoning, and the sparks begin to fly between the terminals. The bridge so laboriously built, no longer needed, is just kicked into the stream. Then he jumps. ...

We in the West are growing used to Kierkegaard and his "existential leap", and it is but the jump of Zen. You may, if you wish, be dramatic about it. Drag yourself with the last ounce of your intellect to the jaws of the abyss. Thought can go no further;

[1] *Perennial Philosophy,* pp. 106 and 113.
[2] *Living by Zen,* p. 95.

heaven lies beyond. With the last gasp of the whole soul's will (that doesn't sound right somehow) ... or you can meditate on one of the most famous *haiku* in Japan.

> *The old pond.*
> *A frog jumps in—*
> *Plop!*

What, then, is satori, which lies at the end of the plop? There is, of course, no answer to this question. As Walt Whitman wrote:

> *"When I undertake to tell the best I find I cannot,*
> *My tongue is ineffectual on its pivots,*
> *My breath will not be obedient to its organs,*
> *I become a dumb man."*

"The Tao that can be expressed is not the eternal Tao," and satori cannot be handed over from one man to another. It is absolutely personal and not repeatable, nor in any way communicable to others. Can I tell you what I feel when I listen to Bach's B Minor Mass, or watch Danilova in *Lac des Cygnes,* or the dawn in the Indian desert? We can speak of the approach and the results of satori, but seldom with profit of its nature. But we can try.

Let us for the moment enter the world of Buddhist philosophy and there rush up the ladder of the intellect and then jump off. Dr. W. McGovern[1] and Dr. Suzuki[2] have both described for us in detail the supreme discovery of the Kegon school of Buddhism. Jijimuge (lit: "things, things unimpeded"), "the unimpeded interdiffusion of all particulars", is just conceivable by the intellect, but only the intuition can understand it. Ji are things, events, the concrete and particular, while Ri is the principle, reason, the abstract, the totality. Ji is discrimination; Ri is non-discrimination, non-distinction. Ri equates with *sunyata,* the Plenum-Void, and Ji with *rupam,* form.

The relationship of Ri and Ji is "perfect, unimpeded mutual solution" (*en-yu-muge*). Ri = Ji and Ji = Ri. They are modes or aspects of an undivided unity. They are mutually in a perpetual state of "suchness".

Now all Ji being Ri, if A = x and B = x, then A = B, and A as an apple and B as a boat are one. This is Rijimuge, the interdiffusion of all Ji with Ri. But the relation between A and B is still indirect, i.e., via the common denominator, Ri. Thus the doctrine of Rijimuge, propounded by the Tendai School of Buddhism, is not even the highest conceivable, much less the highest in truth. The Kegon School went further, and insisted on direct relation between all "things", which, in the Buddhist sense, are seen as flowing events or minor whirlpools on the surface of becoming. Rijimuge seeks the Buddha (the universal) in the individual mind, the body being the devil whose limitations prison the wings of spirit; Jijimuge, on the other hand, the final stage of the Kegon School (and thought can go no further), with its doctrine of the *direct* interdiffusion of all Ji, means finding the Universal Buddha in every particular thing. The implications of this doctrine are enormous. In the words of Hindu philosophy, "Thou art THAT," and all other "thou's" are equally THAT. So far the mind can follow with ease. But according to Jijimuge all "thou's", or apples or boats, are not only THAT but *directly* each other, completely and altogether. Two points on the circumference of a circle, instead of merely looking to the self-same centre, *are* at the centre all the time. This means, of course, that the circle folds up, as it were, into the Void of the Unmanifest. So it does, and why be fearful at the thought of it? But the Universe is manifest for a while on the cross of Space and Time, and meanwhile the circle (whose centre is nowhere and its circumference everywhere) is the field of the world around us. But though the intellect can just conceive that things are directly one, they never cease for a moment (still less for the Absolute Moment) to be, as Zen with a maddening grin points out, their own incomparable selves. Thus the apple is an apple none the less for being a boat, and the boat is a boat for all its appleness, or grand-piano-ness or cup-of-tea-dom.

And the application of all this? The Zen Master dwells on such a plane when he faces his stuggling pupils. The world is filled with boats and apples, and they see them; and he sees them too. The world is also filled with pairs of opposites, like male and female, Tory and Labour, raining-like-hell and a clear fine day, and they see them all; and he sees them too, but he sees them as the two sides of a coin and is quite indifferent to their difference.

But this is not all. Zen is accused of being cold, of lacking a heart. Nothing is more untrue. As already set out, Zen has no philosophy, but adopts what it chooses of other schools, and uses it. As Dr. Suzuki says, "There are two pillars supporting the great edifice of Buddhism, *Mahaprajna*, the Great Wisdom, and

Mahakaruna, the Great Compassion. The Wisdom flows from the Compassion and the Compassion from the Wisdom, for in fact the two are one, though from the human point of view, we have to speak of them as two."[1] In the world of Jijimuge, therefore, when you and I are one, even though we never cease to be ourselves, why prate of compassion or love for one's fellow men? Love, as I said to myself when far too young, is a cosmic glue; it sticks together the parts of the whole until we realise that, being one, they don't need sticking together. I even wrote a (no doubt) turgid poem to the effect that one day love itself will die, when people realise that, like God, it is a superfluous idea. He who has even glimpsed the sunlight of Jijimuge just KNOWS himself to be one with all humanity, all things, all life, and acts accordingly; those who do not know resort to a God or the "charity" bazaar.

One morning in bed I thought that I understood all this, but I doubt if I can put it into words. My reasoning went like this, but you must make for yourselves the jump at the end of it.

Two bodies, even in passionate embrace, never mingle. The skin is never broken; each remains an undivided entity. Think this out, for it is true. "Their hearts entwine." Nonsense, they no more interfuse emotionally, in the sense that they cease to be what they are, than two cushions laid on one another. "Their minds are one." They are not, and no man has the least idea of the inmost thoughts of his dearest friend. But they share a proportion of thoughts and emotions, react in the same way to the same events, and according to the occult tradition their "mental bodies" intermingle. For there is no life without form, and the mind must have its "body" or definite form as much as a football ground. Go higher; let our two friends each develop the intuition so that they now communicate to a large extent in silence. They are growing one on this highest human plane of consciousness, but even as they grow into the "no-mind" (*mu-shin*) of satori, they never cease to be what they are, Mr. and Mrs. Brown. Go on, go higher still; purify the "bodies" of our friends as in ever purer relationship they grow together and one with all humanity. Can you now feel the oneness of all "things" while they, no whit less what they severally are, are fused in one—while having tea ... ?

The coming of satori is about as comfortable as an atom bomb in a dug-out. "Ever since the unfoldment of consciousness we have been led to respond to the inner and outer conditions in a certain

[1] *The Essence of Buddhism*, p. 40.

conceptual and analytical manner. The discipline of Zen consists
in upsetting this ground-work once for all and reconstructing the
old frame on an entirely new basis."[1] The crisis is usually violent.
"Satori is the sudden flashing into consciousness of a new truth
hitherto undreamed of. It is a sort of mental catastrophe taking
place all at once, after much piling up of matters intellectual and
demonstrative. The piling has reached the limit of stability and the
whole edifice has come tumbling to the ground when, behold, a
new heaven is open to full survey."[2] The will becomes fused with
the principle of Enlightenment and, weary of the shackles of
thought and feeling, suddenly throws the last of its fetters away.
The whole being of the man is involved, and the transformation or
"conversion" is complete. ... The perceiving I is in one sense
unaltered. It still sees the morning paper that it knows so well, and
the bus to the office remains unaltered, but the perceiver and the
perceived have merged into one, and the two-ness of things has
gone. The continuum of sense experience, to resort to modern
jargon, is now undivided; we see the film in one instead of as a
series of pictures, and the change is not only psychological, as to
our "seeing", but metaphysical, as to our understanding of all
relationship. The undifferentiated totality of things is, as it were,
understood from inside; the viewpoint is now from the centre of
things and not from some ever-changing point on the wheel. "This
state of no-mind exists, as it were, on a knife-edge between the
carelessness of the average sensual man and the strained over-
eagerness of the zealot for salvation. To achieve it, one must walk
delicately and, to maintain it, must learn to combine the most
intense alertness with a tranquil and self-denying passivity, the
most indomitable determination with a perfect submission to the
leadings of the spirit."[3] Aldous Huxley has got the paradox all
right, but has he got the satori of which the paradox is the only
possible expression?

Satori is seeing into one's own nature, and this nature is not our
own. It is on the contrary, Nature, or, if one must add labels to it,
Buddha-nature, and it does not belong to you or me. It dwells in
what Dr. Suzuki calls "the Absolute Present". You will remember
the story of the wild geese flying overhead. The Master asked,
"What are they?" The pupil answered, "Wild geese, Master."

[1] *Introduction to Zen Buddhism*, p. 99.
[2] *Ibid*, p. 100.
[3] *Perennial Philosophy*, p. 86.

"Whither are they flying?" "They are all gone now." The pupil got a tweak on the nose and cried aloud in pain. "Are they really gone?" asked the Master. The pupil gained satori. To show that he now "understood", he waited till the Master began his sermon in the Zen-Do, and then went forward and rolled up the Master's mat, which means the end of the session. The Master left his seat and went to his room. He sent for the pupil and asked him why he had rolled up the mat. "My nose does not hurt me any more today," said the pupil. "How well you understand 'today'," said the Master, satisfied. Commenting upon this, Dr. Suzuki says, "The birds are in space and fly in time; you look at them and you put yourself immediately in space-relations; you observe they are flying, and this at once confines you in the frame of time. Thus you step off the Absolute Present, which means that you are no more a free, self-regulating spirit but a mere man, karma-fettered and logically-minded."[1] We must learn to see those birds before they enter the realm of birth and death, of space and time, nor cease to admire them so as the wife calls out that tea is ready. Then only has the skin fallen off, as a Master described his satori, baring the One-true-substance-only. Nor shall we fail to know when the moment arrives, for its power is enormous, and if Jove wielded a thunderbolt it was not more dangerous than Zen.

All this, it may be said, can be paralleled in Europe. So it can, for satori is no respecter of persons, and knows nothing at all of East and West, of Buddhism, agnosticism or Christianity. William James, in *The Varieties of Religious Experience,* has collated a large and authentic collection of such experiences, and the Canadian psychiatrist, Dr. R. M. Bucke, produced in 1901 his famous *Cosmic Consciousness,* in which the subject was reviewed anew. In modern times Dr. Kenneth Walker's *Diagnosis of Man* has again approached the subject, and the field is too vast to be here surveyed. I can serve the occasion better by providing material from the East for a later comprehensive survey. But just as the "mind" is immensely complex, including as it does all parts of the man, from the almost physical etheric plane to the, however small it be, flame of Enlightenment, so "religious" experiences are of a huge variety. From St. Paul's "suddenly there shined around him a light from heaven", to Dr. Bucke's own remarkable experiences, the essence is the same. There must be a background providing an emotional or mental tension. Then comes the flash,

[1] *Living by Zen,* p. 62.

or it may be an hour's experience of varying intensity; then when
the vision fades there is the eager but useless attempt to explain it
to others. St. Paul's was a light which shined around. Dr. Bucke, in
his hansom cab, "found himself wrapped around as it were by a
flame-coloured cloud, which was followed by an intellectual
illumination quite impossible to describe."[1] The late Sir James
Crichton-Browne could induce it by a well-known method of self-
hypnosis. He would repeat his own name to himself, silently, until
"as it were out of the intensity of the consciousness of
individuality, individuality itself seemed to dissolve and fade away
into boundless being, and this not a confused state but the clearest,
the surest of the surest, utterly beyond words—where death was an
almost laughable impossibility—the loss of personality (if it were
so) seeming no extinction, but the only true life".[2] Is this delusion?
Tennyson, who had the same experience, did not think so. "By
God Almighty! there is no delusion in the matter! It is no nebulous
ecstasy, but a state of transcendent wonder, associated with
absolute clearness of mind."[3] Had he at this time written *The
Mystic*, that superb and much-neglected poem? Another poet,
Rupert Brooke, has described the experience in his *Dining-Room
Tea*. Time stood still.

> "The tea
> Hung on the air, an amber stream;
> I saw the fire's unglittering gleam
> The painted flame, the frozen smoke. ...."

With Edward Carpenter it was the stone Buddha that came to life.
Of the traveller who "took Pansil" before the Buddha image in the
ruined city of Anuradhapura he wrote, "His thoughts subside, like
waves on water when the wind ceases. He too for a moment
touches the well-spring of being—he swims into identity with the
universe; the trees flicker in the evening light, the Buddha just gives
the slightest nod, as much as to say, 'That's it,' and then—he is but
stone again and the road stretches beyond."[4] Some have had the
experience under or recovering from an anæsthetic, when
consciousness was for a moment freed from the fleshly envelope.
Dr. Kenneth Walker tells of a patient shouting while coming

[1] *Cosmic Consciousness*, p. 8.
[2] *The Varieties of Religious Experience*, p. 384.
[3] *Ibid*, p. 384.
[4] *Adam's Peak to Elephanta*, p. 108.

round, "You don't understand, you don't understand. No one
understands. The Universe ... the universe. I know, I know!
Happiness is within you. You don't have to look outside, it's
within you. ..."¹ He, too, had found the "Absolute Moment". Mr.
Winston Churchill's experience as he came out of an anæsthetic
was more intellectual, yet obviously approaches satori. "I see the
absolute truth and explanation of things, but something is left out
which upsets the whole, so by a larger sweep of the mind I have to
see a greater truth and a more complete explanation, which
comprises the erring element. Nevertheless there is still something
left out. So we have to take a still wider sweep. ... The process
continues inexorably. Depth upon depth of unendurable truth
opens." If I venture to mention three of my own experiences it is
only to show the variety that one mind may experience.

I was having tea alone with the cat on my lap, and a "tea-time"
programme on the wireless to relax my mind after a session of
writing this book. I suddenly felt very happy, an unusual state in
my intensely active and imaginative mind, then, as it were, I felt
about me a steadily rising tide of enormous joy. I wanted to sing,
or to dance to the music. The warmth of the tide was glorious, as of
a huge affectionate flame. I remained intellectually conscious; that
is, I was critical of my own condition, considering it, comparing it,
wondering what it might mean. Never before had I attained this
discriminate consciousness which functions on a plane where all
discrimination seemed absurd. Then the tide ebbed slowly and I
was left exhilarated, rested, refreshed.

A far more prolonged experience took place in Kyoto. I went for
the weekend from my work in Tokyo, and only on a return visit a
fortnight later did I realise the condition of mind in which I had
spent the entire weekend. It was the climax of an attempt to draw
together various Japanese sects on the "Twelve Principles of
Buddhism", the birth of which I described in *Via Tokyo*. I was
probably worked up to the importance of the occasion, but when I
arrived at the all-important meeting, and was faced with fifty
distinguished Buddhist abbots and monks from all over Japan, I
suddenly dropped all mental content, all emotion, and sat, without
thinking what I was to say, in a state of almost absurd serenity. I
was no longer interested in results, nor anxious, nor proud, nor at
all concerned with self. I was utterly happy, perfectly serene, and

¹ *Diagnosis of Man*, p. 158.
² Quoted *Ibid*, p. 158.

above all magnificently certain. I *knew* what I had to say and do; I *knew* that it was right. I felt but a cog in an infinitely complex process of becoming, wherein I just played what I knew to be my part. There was neither emotion nor thought; all differences were healed in wholeness. There was a light within me as well as the sunlight filtering through the bamboo curtains on to the golden floor. When I spoke, I am told that I spoke "as one having authority". In the end all agreed to what I had asked, but I did not react to any victory. I just went on to the next appointment, a pleasant dinner with friends which I enjoyed enormously. Only a fortnight later, when I met the same group of men and tried to settle details with them did I find that I was arguing. The vision was gone, and with it the certainty. I was back in the world of the opposites and I was on one side.

A third type of experience, and indeed my first, had no immediate "background" and I was in fact in a Turkish bath. Suddenly, as I lay at physical and mental ease, there was a blinding flash of vision, a lightning flash that "held" for several seconds of time. I understood at last, completely and beyond all argument, the whole problem of self and selfishness, of suffering and the cause of suffering, of desire and the ending of desire. Like a fool I tried to explain the vision to myself, and of course it fled.

None of these examples, of famous men or my own, has any concern with God. Satori is utterly impersonal, draws all its powers under a central wing and stands like a rock on its own foundation. It is sufficient unto itself, its own authority. It is utterly here and now and "this", and takes no thought for the morrow. Without any sense of separateness there is no need of benevolence, or of love for one's fellow men. When I and my Father are one, why seek that One?

Is satori a sudden or gradual achievement; and is it complete in itself, in the sense that you have or have not achieved satori, or are there stages and degrees of enlightenment? In the course of my studies I have found what seem to be opposite opinions on these related questions, and it may be useful to summarise the apparent differences and attempt to review them, as all opposites, in the light of satori.

Historically, it was the Patriarch Wei Lang who, in the seventh century, called his School the "Sudden" School, as distinct from Shin-shao's School of Gradual Attainment. The distinction, according to Wei Lang, is solely one of speed. "While there is only one system of law (Dharma), some disciples realise it more quickly than others. The reason why the names 'Sudden' and 'Gradual' are given is that some disciples are superior to others in mental disposition. So far as the Dharma is concerned, the distinction of 'Sudden' and 'Gradual' does not exist."[1] Huang Po says much the same thing. "The realisation of universal mind (satori) may come slowly or quickly. There are those who upon hearing this Dharma, rid themselves of mentation in a single flash of thought. Others accomplish the same thing through the Ten Beliefs, the Ten Stages ..." etc. In other words, Zen is the path which runs straight up the hill-side to the top. It is im-mediate, without donkeys or guides or seats on which to rest at intervals and admire the view.

So far so clear, but how "abrupt" is the satori thus gained, and how complete when first experienced? Dr. Suzuki says, "The reason why the Southern School (of Wei Lang) is known as 'abrupt' is because it upholds that the coming of enlightenment is instantaneous and does not allow for any gradation, as there are no stages of progress in it. ..."[2] And again, "The doctrine of abruptness is the result of looking at the multitudinousness of things in absolute unity. All true mystics are followers of the abrupt school. The flight from the alone to the alone is not and cannot be a gradual process. ... As it opens up all of a sudden a world hitherto undreamed of, it is an abrupt and discrete leaping from one plane of thought to another."[3] On the face of it this conflicts with the same author's remarks in an earlier passage, when he says, "To deserve the name satori the mental revolution must be so complete as to make one really and sincerely feel that there took place a fiery baptism of the spirit. The intensity of this feeling is proportional to the amount of effort the opener of satori has put into the achievement. For there is a gradation of satori as to its intensity, as in all our mental activity."[4]

Alan Watts, who learnt nine-tenths of his Zen, as I have, from Dr. Suzuki, thinks that "essentially Satori is a sudden experience, and it is often described as a 'turning over' of the mind, just as a pair of scales will suddenly turn over when a sufficient amount of material has been poured into one pan to overbalance the weight in the other."[5]

[1] *Sutra of Wei Lang*, p. 93.
[2] *Essays* I, p. 199.
[3] *Ibid*, p. 200.
[4] *The Eastern Buddhist*, Vol I, p. 210.
[5] *The Spirit of Zen*, p. 68.

So far there is room for confusion between three things, a school of training which aims at direct, im-mediate enlightenment, a rushing straight up the hill, which is undoubtedly the method of Zen; secondly, the violence and utter change of quality in the experience when achieved, which itself is the result of long preparation; and thirdly, the completeness or incompleteness of the experience when first achieved. Let us look at what seem to be contrary opinions to those already expressed.

In the Pali Canon of the Thera Vâda or Southern School of Buddhism we read: "Just as, Brethren, the mighty ocean deepens and slopes gradually down, not plunging by a steep precipice—even so, Brethren, in this Dhamma Discipline the training is gradual, it goes step by step; there is no sudden penetration to insight." That seems clear enough, and it accords with nature, such as the movement of the tide, the opening of a flower, the growth from childhood to maturity. And there is Zen "authority" for it. "When one is earnest enough," said a monk who attained satori, "realisation will come to one frequently, and there will be a stripping off at each step forward." And his Master approved of the simile, and said, "The study of Zen is like the polishing of a gem; the more polished the brighter the gem ... when there is the more stripping off of its outer coatings, this life of yours will grow worth more than a gem."[1]

Most western writers on Zen seem to take this view. Mrs. Suzuki, the American wife of Dr. Suzuki, who studied Zen with her husband, says, "In Zen there are grades of realisation ... there is an upward movement in Zen as in everything else, and to solve the first Koan is not the whole by any means."[2] Dr. Pratt, who also studied for a while with Dr. Suzuki, says, "That there are all kinds and degrees of satori can, indeed, hardly be questioned. It is a relative term, and many a good Zen scholar is uncertain whether he has had it or not. When the experience comes in its most intense form it is, indeed, unmistakable, but this intense experience is rare in modern Japan, just as ecstasy is rare in Christendom, and *samadhi* in India." Dr. Pratt was an earnest student of Buddhism in Japan, and the following passage, therefore, must be taken seriously. "It is said that some have experienced satori as many as eighteen times (for it is, of course, a temporary and passing state); but most of those you question will say that they are not sure they

[1] *Essays* II, p. 95.
[2] *Impressions of Mahayana Buddhism*, p. 166.

have ever attained it, though they have approximated it two or three times."[1] In considering these modest opinions, however, it is to be hoped that the learned enquirer bore in mind the amazing self-abnegation of the Japanese, and the fact that it is often said that he who claims to have had satori has not in fact had true satori, for there is still a self to make this foolish claim. "He who knows does not speak; he who speaks does not know."

But that satori in an advanced form is quite rare seems beyond question. Dr. Bucke himself says that the better known members of the group of those whose spiritual eyes have been opened could be collected in a modern drawing-room, but he is speaking of the very top flight of illuminati.[2] Dr. Jung says much the same thing. This is a road, he says, that has been trodden only by a few of our great men—he is speaking, I think, of Westerners. "For a complete experience there can be nothing cheaper or smaller than the whole," and he goes on to describe in the terms of his own psychology why this must be so.

Where, then, in the wide range of "experience" does satori begin? "To merit the name of satori," said Dr. Suzuki in an interview with Steinilber-Oberlin, "the inner revolution must be sufficiently complete for the subject to be really and sincerely conscious that a true baptism has taken place in his mind. The intensity of the sensation is in ratio to the effort by the candidate to satori. For in satori there are different degrees of intensity ... the possessor of a mild satori will not experience the same spiritual revolution as a Rinzai or a Bukko for instance. Zen is an affair of character, not of intelligence."[3]

Where is the truth in all these references? I think Dr. Pratt has found it. The aim of Zen technique, he says, is to jolt the mind out of its accustomed rut and to give the soul such a *bang* that its eyes will be knocked open, and suddenly see the light of an utterly new world. ... "A process of 'incubation' within the subconscious is produced by several months or even years of zazen, meditation, study, training, and 'atmosphere'. When the time is ripe the new insight will exfoliate suddenly from out the subconscious region if only it receives, so to speak, a last shake or stir."[4] W. J. Gabb, the English author of *Beyond the Intellect* and other works on Zen, says the same. All enlightenment is gradual, but its eruption into

[1] *The Pilgrimage of Buddhism*, p. 641.
[2] *Cosmic Consciousness*, p. 9.
[3] *The Buddhist Sects of Japan*, pp. 155-56.
[4] *The Pilgrimage of Buddhism*, p. 632.

consciousness may be sudden in cases where its appearance has been obstructed by an over-active intellect or excess of sensuality.

To most professing Christians the Sermon on the Mount is only a beautiful precept in a beautiful holy frame; it is considered to be ideal as an ideal, but it is not thought to be practicable in the rough and tumble of usual life. But every now and then the truth breaks through the crust of rationalism, and there is a repetition of the phenomenon of religious conversion, analogous to the sudden enlightenment of Zen Buddhism. It may be, therefore, that what was written in *Concentration and Meditation* in 1935 is right. "There are many degrees of satori, ranging from a flash of intuitive understanding to pure Samadhi. Presumably the different grades of koan collate with the grades and levels of satori. First, the purely personal prejudices are discarded, followed by the racial or national points of view. As the koan gets more difficult, the claims of humanity begin to predominate until, at the threshold of Samadhi, the individual consciousness is merged in the Universal Mind. Then only is the unconscious of the individual and the unconscious of the universe made one, and self, bereft of any abiding place, dissolves into nothingness."[1] But I can imagine a Zen Master, if he happened to read that, saying, "Now that you have got that stuff off your chest, go and clean your boots."

To summarise, whether the final assault on satori be swift or slow, in the end we storm the gates of Heaven, and we do not stand in a queue at the entrance filling in forms. When satori is achieved, whether for a second or for an hour, it is violent, cataclysmic, an unmistakable conversion from the old mode of consciousness to a new. The first experience, however, may be short or long, of low or high degree, complete or, far more likely, very incomplete, for the road from a first taste of satori to the Buddha's Supreme Enlightenment must be long indeed. But the gates, once opened, never again completely close, and the satori thereafter is of increasing frequency, length and quality, until the time comes for some measure of control. At first there will be an increasing ability to induce the mood of satori by one means or another; finally comes the power to command it. For only when consciousness can be raised at will to the plane of (comparative) enlightenment, and there maintained at will, does the pilgrim truly enter into his heritage, and "being free he knows that he is free" and mountains are once more mountains and it's time for tea.

[1] P. 247.

Chapter 9

The Results of Satori

The effect of Zen on the arts and culture of China and Japan has already been described; we have now to consider the effects on the man. The effects are, of course, proportionate to the strength of the cause, that is, the degree of satori achieved, for the law of Karma, cause-effect, operates unceasingly.

Some who achieve satori express their experience in a *ge (gatha)*, a poem whose content varies as widely as the "experience" of the poet. It must be remembered that poetry to the Japanese, and to the Chinese before them, is a far more common and far more reverenced mode of expression than with any race in the West. And just as the Abbot of the great Shokoku-ji in Kyoto was able to paint for me a picture of Bodhidharma almost out of hand, so many a student of Zen, on attaining a glimpse of satori, was able to express himself in excellent verse.

A monk called Yenju heard a bundle of fuel drop, and attained satori. At once he composed,

> *"Something dropped! It is no other thing;*
> *Right and left there is nothing earthy.*
> *Rivers and mountains and the great earth,*
> *Revealed in them all is the Body of the Dharmaraja."*[1]

This at least makes sense, but the following is entirely "Zen":

> *"An octagonal mill-stone rushes through the air;*
> *A golden-coloured lion has turned into a cur;*
> *If you want to hide yourself in the North Star,*
> *Turn round and fold your hands behind the South Star."*[2]

But the oldest and most famous *ge* comes from the Pali Canon. It is a curious little story, and being a perfect and early example of the attainment of satori centuries before the Dhyâna (Ch'an, Zen)

---

[1] Lit.: King of the Dharma, the Buddha.
[2] Chosen from others in *Essays* I, pp. 234-35.

School was born, it has always seemed to me strange that neither students of Zen, who are apt to claim satori as their own, nor students of the Thera Vâda, who are apt to sneer at Zen, take heed of it. Sariputta and Moggallana, two Brahmans who later became famous figures in the Buddha's Ministry (their "relics" were returned from England to Sanchi in 1948, to the Stupa whence they had been dug up in the nineteenth century), were disciples of the same Master, and each promised to tell the other as soon as he "attained the Immortal". One day Sariputta met the Venerable Assaji, a distinguished member of the Order. He asked Assaji about his Master's Teaching, but Assaji explained that he was new to the Order, and could not explain the Dhamma in detail. "But tell me the meaning," said Sariputta. "Why make so much of the letter?" The reply was remarkable. Is this indeed the essence of Buddhism?

> "The Buddha hath the cause described
> Of all things springing from a cause;
> And also how things cease to be—
> This is the Great One's Teaching."

Not what the cause is, be it noted, but merely the fact that the cause had been described, and its ceasing. Yet Sariputta, the wandering ascetic, having heard this Dhamma-text, obtained the pure and spotless Dharma-eye, namely, "Whatever is an arising thing, that is a ceasing thing." Thus did Sariputta "attain the Immortal" by a phrase which in the passing of time has been condensed into, "Coming to be, coming to be; ceasing to be, ceasing to be." Sariputta was ripe for satori, and a phrase of philosophy, given him second-hand, was enough to provide the spark for the explosion. In Dr. Suzuki's words, "Sariputta's understanding of the doctrine of 'origination and cessation' was not the outcome of his intellectual analysis but an intuitive comprehension of his inner life-process."[1]

But hundreds of the famous Japanese *hokku*, or *haiku*, a three-line poem of seventeen syllables (5 : 7 : 5), and the slightly longer *tanka* or *uta* thirty-one syllables (5 : 7 : 5 : 7 : 7) are inspired by a minor degree of satori, and are the outcome of a Buddhist training and a Buddhist frame of mind. This is a fact which many a writer on Japanese poetry overlooks. It is true that the subject is generally trivial, and its treatment so delicate, so graceful, so

[1] *Essays* I, p. 59.

utterly refined, that these "pearls to be dissolved in the wine of a mood", as some Englishman has charmingly called them, are far removed from the usual conception of "sacred verse". But Yone Noguchi,[1] who, surprisingly enough, ignores their Buddhist ancestry, agrees that "the hokku poet's chief aim is to impress the readers with the high atmosphere in which he is living", and this high atmosphere is more than a mere cultural refinement; it must include the element of *wabi*, or of *yugen*, that "poverty" of soul in which the intuition can have full display. Basho (1644–94), the most famous poet of Japan, was a Samurai by birth, but went into voluntary exile as a penniless wanderer, living for and in his poetry. His was "an acceptance of the greater happiness which comes to those who follow an ideal".[2] He lived in a world of satori, and his poems came out of it. Perhaps his greatest poem—books have been written about it—has already been quoted in R. H. Blyth's translation. In Japanese it reads.

> *"Furu-ike ya*
> *Kawazu tobi-komu*
> *Mizu no oto."*

Literally it means, "The old pond. A frog leapt into—the sound of water." Blyth's version is genius; transcending all translation he gives us a *haiku* fit to be added to English verse.

> *"The old pond.*
> *A frog jumps in.*
> *Plop!"*

Basho was always direct, concrete, clear; no "modern verse" for him. "When Basho looked at an onion he saw an onion; when he felt a deep, unnameable emotion, he said so. But he did not mix them all up in a vague pantheistic stew or symbolic pot-pourri."[3] And in a Japanese poem there is room to say so little in so few syllables that only a finger pointing to the moon is possible; the moon can never be described.

To talk about the experience of satori is useless. Just as the *haikus* form a living stream of poetry and not a stagnant pool, so one should accept satori, use it, and pass on. "So when things are brought to you, you just accept them and say thank you, but do

[1] *The Spirit of Japanese Poetry*, p. 36.
[2] *The Cloud Men of Yamato*, GATENBY, p. 99.
[3] *Zen in English Literature* ..., BLYTH, p. 58.

not talk about it. Zen tries to make you accept things, and when you have accepted them you give a hearty laugh."[1]

If another denies your satori, let him. Argument is useless. What you know you know, and none shall take it from you.

Apart from futile attempts to describe, to oneself or one's friends, the experience gained, the first result of satori is often more satori, for once the shell has been broken it is not long before the chicken (or the goose in the bottle) is out. Psychologically, as already briefly explained, the result is a second birth or new becoming, for the ego, in the sense of the self which certain Buddhist teachers spend their time persuading their audiences has no existence (*anatta*), receives in satori (and not one moment before) its death-wound, and there is born, on the hypothetical line where the conscious and unconscious meet, the Self which in the end will achieve Supreme Enlightenment. Satori is, therefore, the re-making of life itself, and the fundamental effect on the individual is the test of the genuine nature of the experience. The victorious warrior marches round his mind with a bloodstained battle-axe, and smashes to pieces every conception, dirty or glorious, that he can find, ending with the total destruction of conviction that he has attained satori. Asked, "How shall we attain to freedom," a Master answered, "Who put you under restraint?"

Collating the hints and feeble descriptions of those who have had some measure of satori, one may mention again those qualities or powers which dominate the mind thereafter. They seem to include, though themselves very difficult to describe, certainty, serenity, clarity, and a sense of rhythm, of being part of the instrument of the wholeness of things.

The serenity is glorious.

> "*Imperturbable and serene the ideal man practises no virtue,*
> *Self-possessed and dispassionate, he commits no sin.*
> *Calm and silent he gives up seeing and hearing.*
> *Even and upright his mind abides nowhere.*"[2]

If this is putting it a trifle high for the beginner in satori, at least he begins to see that such a state is possible, and he sees the meaning of the Zen ideal, "Be business-less in mind; be mind-less in business."

[1] *Buddhism in England*, SUZUKI, Vol. XI, p. 69.
[2] *Sutra of Wei Lang*, p. 124.

Emotion largely ceases to cloud the intellect, and the intellect, with its host of prejudices, loses its power to cloud the intuitive judgment. Worry, the product of doubt and desire, dies with its parents; the inward and outward are equalised. As Keyserling remarked, of the Abbot Soyen Shaku of Kamakura, the author of *Sermons of a Buddhist Abbot*, "I have never yet had such an impression of inwardness, coupled with equal martial energy"[1] and W. G. Moore, in his review of Iremonger's *William Temple*, after speaking of the Archbishop's energy, remarks, "It is a strange thing that one so busy should have impressed so many people by his ... serenity ... The intensity of his prayer life seems to have enabled him to conquer pain and friction and fatigue. It all seemed very breathless but he was never out of breath." The same applies to the great men whom I have had the privilege to meet. The Ven. Tai Hsü of China, the spiritual reformer of Chinese Buddhism; Nicholas Roerich, the Russian painter, explorer, poet and idealist; Meher Baba, the apostle of pure love which radiates from him as the warmth of a spiritual fire; and Jamshed Nasserwanji, the saint-like business-man of Karachi who, nine times its mayor, built most of the modern city: all these four men, and their lives could hardly be more various, had the quality of high serenity, and only those who have sat at the receiving end, so to speak, of Dr. Suzuki's mind can speak of his power to lift the receiver's mind a long way to the level of his own. Keyserling had an enormous mind, and at least it was brightly illumined with the approaching rays of satori, and Jung of Zurich has a mind whose range and power and spiritual strength are not yet commonly perceived. I venture to prophesy, however, that one day he will be recognised as one of the first to bridge, as only the intuition and never the intellect can bridge, the chasm which all too effectively divides the man-created spheres of "East" and "West".

As for the "finished product", the master of life, Tennyson has given in *The Mystic*, one of his greatest and least known poems, the finest description of such a man, whose occult powers and state of awareness have alike been raised to the highest human degree. Such a man may be as nothing in the eyes of men. His power lies in what he is, not in his influence on the outward lives of men. What we do is what we are; when we are, we shall know what to do. But until we develop the faculty of direct, im-mediate vision into realities we shall not recognise these men. Deep calls to deep; our

[1] *Travel Diary of a Philosopher*, Vol. II, pp. 227–28.

shallow minds may fail to recognise the deeps which we so glibly describe, yet know not.

> *"Ye knew him not: he was not one of ye,*
> *Ye scorned him with an undiscerning scorn:*
> *Ye could not read the marvel in his eye,*
> *The still serene abstraction: he hath felt*
> *The vanities of after and before;*
> *Albeit, his spirit and his secret heart*
> *The stern experiences of converse lives,*
> *The linked woes of many a fiery change*
> *Had purified, and chastened, and made free."*

There follows a remarkable description of the four *Kumaras*, the "Regents of the Earth" whose existence is well known to eastern philosophy. And then:

> *"How could ye know him? Ye were yet within*
> *The narrower circle; he had wellnigh reached*
> *The last, which with a region of white flame,*
> *Pure without heat into a larger air*
> *Upburning, and an ether of black blue,*
> *Investeth and ingirds all other lives."*

These men have the Absolute Moment, or an increasing sense of it. There is such a thing as the sacrament of the moment, and all should be offered to it. The higher consciousness is ever fetching back to the centre the wandering intellect which, for all its boast of seeking truth, will wrap up pieces of it and hide them away in splendid concepts, as a dog will bury a bone instead of eating it. "The will is the man himself, and Zen appeals to it," but behind will stands desire, as the occult saying runs. Zen is a harnessing of the will to universal purposes, "attaching one's belt to the Power-House of the Universe," as Trine has called it somewhere. But the use which is made of this power depends on desire, and only the character of the man can say if the desire be that of the selfish or the selfless side of the driver of the machine. But the man of satori has learnt to relax desire, to "let go" into non-discrimination and no-purpose. He just lets go and enjoys the serenity of letting go, of relaxing the tension of personal desire which causes, as the Buddha proclaimed, the great "sea of suffering" which all but engulfs mankind. As I have often felt, this holding apart the things which in fact are one is all very tiring! How delightful and how restful to summon the energy to drop it, as a piece of elastic drawn to its limits, and then—"let go!"

The sense of certainty, already described, is no less glorious, and it comes very often as a negative absence of doubt. There is nothing aggressive about it, and it seems to be linked with the "experience of transparency" of which Dr. Suzuki speaks. Referring to the Japanese love of nature, he says, "As long as we harbour conceptual illusions arising from the separation of subject and object as final, the transparency is obscured, and our love of nature is contaminated with dualism and sophistry."[1] Irrationalities now make sense; they are clearly seen through as the two sides of a piece of glass. "Black is white and white is black" becomes, from bosh, a simple statement of fact, and, "How is it that a man of great strength cannot lift his legs?" is easy to answer. Moreover, with a greater vision of things as they are, we lose our habit of slapping on labels in the belief that the thing is changed or our understanding of it is thereby improved. But the weather remains the weather and your neighbour's wireless your neighbour's wireless, whether your label attached to it be printable or unprintable; and Zen is Zen, no more or less, for the long description you choose to attach, or attempt to attach, to its tail. Things just are, and for the first time in his life the master of satori is content to leave them so.

But, as a friend once said to me, one cannot become extraordinary until one is content to be extra-ordinary, and it seems that it needs a touch of satori before the average man will let go of his ego-phantasy, the belief that he matters in the least, and become what he is, just a drop in the ocean or a grain of sand on its shore. With satori, mountains are once more mountains, and a man but a man, just one particular in the inter-diffusion of all particulars which is Jijimuge. The paradoxes of Zen are thrown away; the koan and mondo are rafts which have borne us to the further shore; they are no more needed. The goose can stay in the bottle, for all we care, and the geese just fly away.

But this serenity, and certainty, and sense of rhythm only begin to operate when satori has not only moved into the mind but has settled down to stay. One flash has no immediate effect on character. Many a man who has known satori is, to his neighbour, none the better for it, but in time the change appears. One of the first results is that rarest of all virtues, genuine humility, and the

[1] *Zen Buddhism and Its Influence*, p. 230.

possessor of satori will neither claim it nor pro-claim it as his own. "Be humble and you will remain entire," is a truth to him, and he climbs no self-erected tower. "Self-gratulation, O Lanoo, is like unto a lofty tower up which a haughty fool has climbed. Thereon he sits in prideful solitude; and unperceived by any but himself."[1] For what has he gained that he should boast of it? Rather he should be abashed that he had not found himself before. There is here no question of acquiring merit, or even of happiness.

There is here no question of morality. Zen consciousness is a mind made one with life, and even at its lowest produces a sense of one-ness with all humanity. Who, having this, needs rules of morality? "The Vinaya rules of conduct" (of the Southern School), says Dr. Suzuki, "are useful and praiseworthy, and when the monks lead their lives in accordance with them they will certainly be good Buddhists. But when the Vinaya cannot go further than regulating one's outward behaviour, they will surely become an undesirable impediment to one's spiritual development."[2] Yet all of us need some discipline for a while, and the monkish life in particular sees to it that the mental strain of the search for satori does not lead to excess. When satori comes, however, the sense of awareness of the rhythm of life will provide its own laws. Coleridge had the right idea. "No work of true genius dares want its appropriate form, neither indeed is there any danger of this. As it must not, so genius cannot, be lawless; for it is ever this that constitutes its genius—the power of acting creatively under laws of its own origination."[3]

When satori has become a sufficiently deep and common experience for the inner change to affect substantially the outer man, he will, while obeying the laws of the land and the customs of his neighbours, live in his spiritual life according to an inner voice, the "voice of the silence", obedience to which, to one whose life henceforth is self-less and purpose-less, is its own reward. But it would seem that a man can have gained a considerable measure of satori without acquiring the power to control it. For a long time satori just comes as it will, without reference to the appropriateness of the occasion. Certainly my own most vivid experience was in a Turkish bath, while on occasions when I needed all the wisdom I could command I have found myself in a flat and positively

[1] *The Voice of the Silence.*
[2] *Living by Zen*, p. 97.
[3] Quoted in *A Poet's Notebook*. EDITH SITWELL, p. 26.

peevish state of mind. Only when consciousness can be raised at will and held at the level of satori, that is, beyond discrimination and conceptual thought, does it become a tool in the hands of a master-craftsman; and satori is, I believe, no more than a tool, though the noblest, perhaps, in the use of the perfect man. Even when control is acquired, and this "direct seeing into the heart of man" and of all situations can be turned on like a tap, the Master does not dwell in it all day. As the Master K. H. wrote to A. P. Sinnett, when explaining much of these matters, "An adept—the highest as well as the lowest—is one only during the exercise of his occult powers."[1]

Nor does the attainment of satori in itself create a Master of Zen. It is one thing to acquire a thorough knowledge of the ways of Zen; quite another thing to live a life which expresses that understanding. There follows, therefore, a period of "maturing", when the would-be Master builds into the tissue of character the food of satori. Where he lives during this introvert digestion is his own affair. It may be alone in the mountains; it may be in the market place. But wherever he lives and however he passes his days, the student, for so he is, is stamping out the last traces of that self whose selfish desires for so long stood in the way of the whole man's enlightenment. Now is the last great battle against the "great dire heresy of Separateness that weans thee from the rest".

As *The Voice of the Silence* warns us, "Kill out desire; but if thou killest it, take heed lest from the dead it should again arise." The lower, personal, separative self will not die willingly, and concept will encumber the path to the last step of the Way. And the sign of self is ever the same, desire. And desire is a veil about the face of Zen.

[1] *The Mahatma Letters to A. P. Sinnett*, p. 180.

Chapter 10

Zen in English Literature

This chapter is inspired by and based upon R. H. Blyth's *Zen in English Literature and Oriental Classics*, of which, I regret to say, I know of only three copies in England, two in the Library of the Buddhist Society, London, and a third which the author gave me in Japan.[1] In the course of its 450 pages, the author displays a knowledge of English Literature and of Zen which no other one man can possess. In a single chapter on the subject, therefore, I can but acknowledge the source of my inspiration; the quotations from the poets, however, are for the most part my own.

Witness to the frequency of satori in western life has already been given in "The Results of Satori". A great many more examples could be given, although it is always difficult to assess the spiritual experience described, and to place it fairly in the field of "mysticism". Not all experiences of a super-normal consciousness are satori, and the serpent of psychic illusion lies at the heart of every flower. Thus Wordsworth's famous lines on Tintern Abbey describe satori.

> *"A sense sublime*
> *Of something far more deeply interfused,*
> *Whose dwelling is the light of setting suns,*
> *And the round ocean and the living air,*
> *And the blue sky, and in the mind of man. . . ."*

Note the word "interfused", which Dr. Suzuki has chosen to describe, if that were possible, the meaning of Jijimuge. On the other hand, Vaughan's vision in "The World" is second-hand. He saw "Eternity like a great Ring of pure and endless light, all calm as it was bright . . ." and the vision is wrought into a glorious poem. But he was still looking *at* something, albeit subjectively, whereas in satori there is no more seer and seen. Whitman found the certainty of satori.

[1] Now obtainable from time to time at the Buddhist Society (1956).

"*I mind how once we lay ...*
Swiftly arose and spread around me the peace and
  knowledge that pass all the argument of the earth,
And I know that the hand of God is the promise of my
  own,
And I know that the spirit of God is the brother of my own,
And that all the men ever born are also my brothers
  and the women my sisters and lovers,
And that a kelson[1] of the creation is love."[2]

Nelson had the serenity of satori, as well as the certainty. "Perhaps the real meaning of the 'Nelson Touch' lies in its certainty, the power he had of inspiring all who met him with the impossibility of his failing in any attempt he made; once a plan had his seal upon it history was already made, even before the event."[3] Those who believe that satori can only come to a man of peace must face this fact, as also the many accounts of soldiers who, in the thick of battle, felt an impersonal exhilaration, a serenity and peace, which they had never known in the office or factory. And Nelson was not always so. He assumed the robe of satori when he became, and because he became, the tool of an impersonal force which, for want of a better word, I call life's pattern or plan. Ashore he was at the mercy of his emotions; at sea almost a god, acting from the impersonal plane of Jijimuge. Just before Trafalgar, when he knew quite well that he would win, and also that he would die, he was "calm and elated". Here is the serenity of satori, and he was not troubled with emotion when he said to his Captain, "God bless you, Blackwood, I shall never see you again."

The poets are even more articulate, for it is their business to find words for that which lies beyond them. Edna St. Vincent Millay in "Renascence" describes an experience which cannot have been mere poet's imagining. High in the landscape, with the earth spread round about her, she lay on her back.

"*The sky, I said, must somewhere stop,*
And—sure enough—I see the top!
The sky, I thought, is not so grand;
I 'most could touch it with my hand!
And reaching up my hand to try,
I screamed to feel it touch the sky.

[1] Keel, or bedplate.
[2] Quoted in *The Varieties of Religious Experience*, JAMES, p. 396.
[3] *Poseidon*, CAPES.

> *"I screamed—and lo!—Infinity*
> *Came down and settled over me. ...."*

Note that infinity pours into her. All mystics, including those who achieve satori, agree that the dew-drop never slips into the Shining Sea, as Edwin Arnold puts it; it is the Shining Sea which pours into the dew-drop. J. C. Squire's experience in "Starlight" was remarkably similar. He too lay in a field and "looked at the stars with lips sealed". Then came the experience,

> *"But through a sudden gate there stole*
> *The Universe and spread in my soul;*
> *Quick went my breath and quick my heart,*
> *And I looked at the stars with lips apart."*

The reference to the "sudden gate" is purely Zen.

But perhaps the essentially Zen experience on which eastern and western poets agree is the absolute value of "trivial" things. When satori comes, all Ji, all things, are equally holy and ultimate. "There is nothing infinite apart from finite things," or, one might add, holy apart from ordinary things. As usual, the poets have it best, for the poet is in love with things, not vague abstractions. "Concrete individual images abound in Zen; in other words, Zen makes use to a great extent of poetical expressions; Zen is wedded to poetry."[1] So were the English, once on a time, before Victorian morality reduced the direct vision of the poet to a mouthing of virtuous abstractions, or the volcanoes of war flung gobbets of the unconscious into our mental life for the "modern" poet to display, without manners or self-discipline, in all their graceless obscenity. And the English will die when they forget poetry. As Flecker writes in *Hassan*,

Caliph: And if there shall ever arise a nation whose people have forgotten poetry or whose poets have forgotten the people, though they send their ships round Taprobane and their armies across the hills of Hindustan, though their city be greater than Babylon of old, though they mine a league into the earth or mount to the stars on wings—what of them?

Hassan: They will be but a dark patch upon the world.

For poets see, and bring their visions, or their satori, to earth as men have need of them. Thus somewhere in English verse the

---

[1] *The Training of the Zen Buddhist Monk*, SUZUKI, p. vii.

major truths of the East have found expression. "Nearly every thought expressed in Buddhist and Hindu literature finds expression in the Western world also; and it could not be otherwise, for the value of these thoughts is universal. The East has advanced beyond the West only in their wider and fuller acceptance."[1] Brave words, and may the West prove worthy of them.

But many a famous poet just misses it. "To see a world in a grain of sand" is excellent mysticism, and splendid pantheism, but it is not Zen. Compare this with Tennyson's "flower in the crannied wall".

> *"If I could understand*
> *What you are, root and all, and all in all,*
> *I should know what God and man is."*

How right he is, for of such is the kingdom of satori. Donne has it too. "God is so omnipresent ... that God is an angel in an angel, and a stone in a stone, and a straw in a straw."[2] He is also a flower in a crannied wall or in a jam-jar.

Good poets, poets worthy of the name, look direct at things. Wrote Whitman:

> *"Stop this day and night with me and you shall possess*
> *the origin of all poems. ...*
> *You shall no longer take things at second or third*
> *hand, nor look through the eyes of the dead, nor*
> *feed on the spectres in books,*
> *You shall not look through my eyes either, nor take*
> *things from me,*
> *You shall listen to all sides and filter them from*
> *yourself."*[3]

The poet sees them for what they are, not as symbols or expressions of something else. As Goethe said, "Do not, I beg you, look for anything behind phenomena. They are themselves their own lessons." This is not materialism; far from it. It is tremendous Zen. No symbolism or simile or analogy is needed in Zen.

> *"The firefly:*
> *As it dropped from a leaf*
> *It suddenly flew away."*

---

[1] *Buddha and the Gospel of Buddhism*, COOMARASWAMY, p. 257.
[2] JOHN DONNE, Sermon VII.
[3] From *Song of Myself*.

Thus Basho's lovely *haiku*: yet analogy is still permitted. Thus Davies,

> *"Butterflies will make side-leaps,*
> *As though escaped from nature's hand*
> *Ere perfect quite."*[1]

How far more satisfactory these concrete poems are than odes to large abstractions like Duty and Beauty and Higher Thought! "Followers of identity and tranquillity are to be given the warning; they are ridden by concepts; let them rise to facts and live in and with them."[2]

"I come in the little things, saith the Lord." How true!

> *"I come in the little things,*
> *Saith the Lord:*
> *Yea! on the glancing wings*
> *Of eager birds, the softly pattering feet*
> *Of furred and gentle beasts, I come to meet*
> *Your hard and wayward heart. ..."*[3]

"Life is sweet, brother. ... There's night and day, brother, both sweet things; sun, moon and stars, brother, all sweet things; there's likewise a wind on the heath." But lest this verges on the merely charming, let us add to Borrow, "there is also toast for tea and the smell of the dust-bin next door"—which are equally things, whether we slap on them the labels of sweet or otherwise.

English poets know, too, of Zen's immediacy, of its sense of the absolute moment. In Arthur Symons' "Credo" we find,

> *"For of our time we lose so large a part*
> *In serious trifles, and so oft let slip*
> *The wine of every moment, at the lip*
> *Its moment, and the moment of the heart."*

But when is a trifle important or unimportant? The answer is clear: When the goose is out of the bottle.

And our poets know of "here". As W. J. Gabb explains,

---

[1] Both quoted in BLYTH, p. 148.
[2] *Zen Buddhism and Its Influence*, p. 233.
[3] *Immanence*, EVELYN UNDERHILL.

> *"Seek and ye shall find.*
> *There is nothing to be found;*
> *But here is a cart;*
> *Look, the wheels go round.*
>
> *Walk a thousand miles—*
> *There is always a beyond;*
> *But here is a frog—*
> *Here, beside the pond. ...."*

And they know of "poverty", that void in the centre of things which only Zen can fill. As Wordsworth wrote,

> *"To sit without emotion, hope or aim,*
> *In the loved presence of my cottage fire,*
> *And listen to the flapping of the flame,*
> *Or kettle whispering its faint undersong."*

Yet how much better is Kyorai's,

> *"'Yes, yes!' I answered,*
> *But someone still knocked*
> *At the snow-mantled gate."*

But the counting of words is foolishness. As Blyth points out, "Words are many and the thing is one, but somehow it has got to be portrayed or suggested in words—but as a unity, not after the post-mortem of thought, not after the dissection of the intellect."[1] Even the seventeen syllables of the Japanese *haiku* may be too many. But the cutting out of unnecessary words or brush-strokes leaves more room for Zen, and few poems written could not be improved by cutting, thereby leaving room for the reader to add his own experience.

Zen lives in humour. It is not humorous and it is not serious; it is Zen, but wit is born from the higher ranges of the mind, where the intuition tries its wings, and humour lies on the razor-edge of self and selflessness, where a man looks round at the back of his head and lifts himself up by his belt. Nonsense, in the sense of Lear's original Limericks, is ever on the verge of Zen, whereas Butler's *Erewhon* is inverted but perfectly sound logic. But meditate on this anonymous jewel,

[1] BLYTH, p. 412.

> "*As I was going up the stair*
> *I met a man who wasn't there,*
> *He wasn't there again today.*
> *I wish to God he'd go away!*"

Alice, of course, whether in Wonderland or through the Looking-Glass, is full of Zen, and did she not, after filling herself with the White Knight's glorious nonsense (to purge her mind of the last grain of "sense"), run down the hill (go over the precipice), to the edge of the brook, and bound across ("crossing the stream"), and throw herself down (complete "letting go"), on a lawn soft as moss, and find on her head the golden crown of satori? All right, she didn't.

But cannot western poets write *haiku*? There is, of course, the language difficulty. Japanese *haiku* are written in Chinese, for though the ideographs are differently pronounced in China and Japan they are formed the same. And the Chinese language, being monosyllabic, is terse and vigorous, and therefore suited to Zen. The overtones and undertones of a series of such ideographs is infinite, and more can be said in a given space than in any other tongue. English is in comparison cumbersome, and even the epigram of two or three lines is usually the brief expression of a "point", witty, satirical or otherwise. A *haiku* has no point; nor does it strive to be beautiful. It is in Zen the expression of the Zen state of mind, and merely points at the moon; it does not attempt to describe it. In itself it has no value; it is not to be parsed, or "analysed", as the beauty of English poems is torn in shreds by an age that knows not the meaning of poetry. The *haiku* is a means, not an end, a hint of the unspeakable. The western poets attempt to describe what they see, or feel, or think. The *haiku* helps you to grasp the sensation direct, as a means or device for "seeing into the soul of man".

I wait for a western poet to turn his hand to a Zen *haiku*. Mr. Kenneth Yasuda, with the pen-name of Shoson, has attempted, in *A Pepper-pod*, not only to translate *haiku* from the Japanese, but to write a few in English. He gives them a western touch by adding rhyme.

> "*Shade of summer trees*
> *Almost reaches to my desk*
> *With the gentle breeze.*"

Or,

> *"Autumn evening,*
> *I came into a straight-road*
> *In my travelling."*

These seem to me, however, to be poetry for the sake of writing poetry, and not the poet writing Zen. Nor is the author concerned with Zen. Such as he writes can be flung off minute by minute, and such is a charming evening's pastime for a group of friends. This is not Zen, nor the road to it. I hesitate to stain the virgin snows of English *haiku* of Zen quality, yet someone must begin. The burden is heavy. I needs must strive for simplicity, for "poverty" or "loneliness", and for "transparency". I must not make a description of things, but offer windows through which the reader may look at things which he had not noticed before. As Ryokan wrote,

> *"You say my poems are poetry?*
> *They are not.*
> *Yet if you understand they are not—*
> *Why, then you see the poetry!"*

They must be concrete. The thing itself is the meaning, and is not to be extracted from it, like saccharine from coal-tar. Finally, they should be written fast, as a *sumiye* painting. Just as the *sumiye* sketch, on quickly absorbent paper, permits no correction and no touching-up, so the *haiku* should be born in a moment, and spring complete from the pen.

The form is easy. Seventeen syllables in three lines in the rhythm of 5 : 7 : 5 produces the *haiku* form; the spirit, for our present purposes, must breathe the spirit of Zen. Here is my first attempt.

> *"My kakemono*
> *Bangs the wall. The wall hears not,*
> *Nor the wind, nor I."*

While taking my seat in a London theatre, I wrote,

> *"The rain falls outside;*
> *The orchestra plays inside.*
> *How the stage revolves!"*

This came apropos of nothing;

> *"This is happiness.*
> *Moonlight and the quiet pool*
> *And a sense of now."*

That, I think, is bad, because it describes, and stops. How feeble these are compared with even a translation of Basho!

> *"Along the mountain path*
> *The scent of plum-blossoms—*
> *And on a sudden the rising sun!"*

W. J. Gabb does better than mine in their Zen content, though the form is that of a *ge* rather than a *haiku*. He is describing a moment of satori in a train. "These words floated ready made into my mind."

> *"Seated cross-legged, hands folded on breast,*
> *Reverently he makes bows.*
> *The crowds that jostle him in the train*
> *See him not.*
> *They stir his garments as the breeze stirs the pine.*
> *Framed in the window is a solitary gull, soaring."*[1]

Let me try again.

> *"You may speak of 'left'.*
> *You may also speak of 'right'.*
> *There is no middle."*

This is "mystical" and too abstract. The same applies to the following, though it is an experience which I hope to know:

> *"This diversity—*
> *How exhausting it all is.*
> *But if I let go?"*

This is a little better:

> *"How grateful I am.*
> *Yesterday was my party.*
> *Today comes the snow."*

Well, I will give you my three best so far (though I may write six tonight), and leave it at that.

> *"I sat in the sea;*
> *The running waves of the sea*
> *Went up down, up down."*

---

[1] From an unpublished MS.

This came on the verandah of Dr. Suzuki's house in Japan:

> *"When I crushed a fly*
> *A fish in the sunlit pond*
> *Cried out in pain."*

And this just came to me, of Zen:

> *"Seek for the casket*
> *Enshrined in your deepest self.*
> *Then smash it to bits!"*

I have said nothing of *tanka*, whose lines are five and its rhythm, 5 : 7 : 5 : 7 : 7; but the same rules apply. Nor have I space to deal with the Zen to be found in English prose, though Blyth treats of it mightily. Let me end on a frivolous-serious Zen note.

> *"Sneezing suddenly,*
> *What profound sense of relief!*
> *Such is satori."*

Chapter 11

Zen for the West

Zen is life, and Zen Buddhism is but one of its forms. Zen has always been, in one form or another, a world-power, for, as R. H. Blyth points out, in so far as men *live* at all, they live by Zen. "Wherever there is a poetical action, a religious aspiration, a heroic thought, a union of the Nature within a man and the Nature without, there is Zen. But in Japan," he adds, "where by tradition and training the ego is kept at its smallest and weakest, where every man is a poet, Zen is both universally diffused and finds its greatest exemplars at the present time."[1]

But will they always remain there? It is true that forms, like old wines, travel badly, and such exemplars of Zen as may arise in the West will create and use new forms in which to express, and teach, the nature of and the way to Zen. If, therefore, the West is to adopt and assimilate Zen, in the sense of a direct, dynamic approach to life, o'erleaping the hurdles of ritual, religion and concept which men impose between themselves and the thing they seek, the old wine must find new bottles, and be fitted into the pattern of western prejudice and ways of thought.

The obvious difficulty lies in the absence of Zen masters, nor is there any likelihood that a quantity of those who have attained that long "maturing" which precedes the ability to teach would come to the West and there learn a western language perfectly enough to use it in the transmission of Zen. Dr. Suzuki gives the stages in Zen training as: (1) A preliminary intellectual equipment for the maturing of Zen consciousness. (Zen, save in its earliest stages, can never be "popular".) (2) A strong desire to transcend oneself, that is, the limitations of our humanity. (3) "A master's guiding hand is generally found to open the way there for the struggling soul"; and (4) "A final upheaval takes place," which is called satori.[2] It is clear from this that a Master is needed as a midwife to the new consciousness, and though we all know that, in

[1] BLYTH, p. vii.
[2] *Essays* II, p. 36.

mystical parlance, the master is ultimately to be found within, yet most of us need help to find him. The psychic tension deliberately created by the koan technique, and kept at an even pressure by the Master's mondo and the like, must be controlled, or it may damage or even wreck the mind. Dr. Suzuki himself seems to recognise this. The student of Zen, he says, comes to a crisis in which he does not know what to do. "If he is allowed to go on like this, the mental distraction may end disastrously. Or his experience may fail to attain its final goal, since it is liable to stop short before it reaches the stage of the fullest maturity."[1] The Master is needed to keep the student, blind with his own intensity of purpose, on the rails, and to test his achievement. It is easy to think that a given experience is satori when it is nothing of the kind, and a psychic tension which blows off, as it were, through a wrong, because unnatural, vent may even lead to insanity. "The koan must find its justification in waking students to a state of genuine satori and not a mere psychological condition. Our satori ... must prove itself useful and valuable in our daily life, not only as an individual but as a world citizen. . . ."[2]

For these reasons I do not believe that the koan technique is suitable for public teaching in the West, in the sense that the average student should be encouraged to use it for his own experiments. I do not see, however, that the mondo form of teaching has the same dangers, and the koan principle, shorn of its deliberate raising of psychic tension, is an admirable method of transcending the limitations of our intellectual, conception-littered mind. And no Master is needed to find us a koan. As W. J. Gabb says, "Life sets me koans to solve, and no student needs to rely on the Zen scriptures for a supply. All of us have all we need, right here to hand. The flower in the crannied wall is available to us as readily as it was to Tennyson. What am I? Why am I? What and why is anything at all? There are koans, koans everywhere if we ever stop to think."[3] But these can be used as objects, or rather focal points of attention; as means for paralysing the division-making tendency of the mind, so that the unifying, higher mind may function. Jung's diagram, which divides the comparative functions of the mind into intellect or emotion, and intuition or sense, is here most valuable. The intuition can increasingly

[1] *Essays* II, p. 43.
[2] *Living by Zen*, p. 175.
[3] From an unpublished MS.

illumine the intellect or the emotions, proportionate to its increasing use. We can cultivate the mood of satori, and the virtues which proclaim it. We can even, I maintain, deliberately cultivate the intuition, as a man may train a set of muscles which he has always possessed but has not hitherto much used. The results may be slow, less rapid than the "Sudden" School of Japan, but if the end is attained, what matter the cold illusion of time?

After all, the Chinese genius made from the raw material of Indian Buddhism the Dhyâna or Ch'an school, which endured at its best for five hundred years in China, and as Zen for another five hundred years in Japan. In the same way we can make of Zen a western school of awareness which will equally spring from the Blessed One's Enlightenment. As is said in the *Vimalakirti Sutra*, "When Buddha preaches with one voice, sentient beings have different comprehensions according to their respective stages of life." And as the very essence of Zen is to bind itself to no one form, this principle makes it immortal. I therefore agree with the late Dwight Goddard: "In this Zen form (Buddhism) proved to be indigenous in China, Japan and Korea, and will so prove to be in America and Europe, because it is so elemental, so practical, so inexpensive, so easily tested and proved, that it is at home in every country where men try to think truly and live earnestly."[1]

But if we in the West can do without Zen Masters, still less do we need priests. A priest is a man who stands between God and man. He may be an intermediary, handing the grace of one to the other; he may be an insolent fellow who dares to attempt to stand in any capacity between a man and his own enlightenment. The Zen priest is within; he admits no God to whom to pray, or for whom to perform a magic ritual, or to whom to intercede for his (possibly quite as enlightened) fellow men. Even the Buddha, before the last bridge is crossed, must be "killed", that is, destroyed as a concept in the mind.

It is partly because Buddhism has no Pope, no Rome, no Bible which none must alter and to which all men must kneel, that it has proved the most tolerant religion known to the history of mankind. No Buddhist has ever burnt his neighbour's body for the sake of his (non-existent) soul, nor has there been a "Buddhist", still less that blasphemous phrase, a "holy" Buddhist, war. It has always taught that truth is either relative (all that we know), or absolute (which we cannot know). It never, therefore, claimed the

[1] *Buddhism in England*, Vol. V, p. 114.

unique possession of truth, and never attacked those fellow seekers who held a different view. Asoka, the Buddhist Emperor of India of the third century B.C., proclaimed this tolerance as an Edict, and it is sad that men have forgotten this Buddhist Edict at the present day. "He who does reverence to his own sect, while disparaging the sects of others ... with intent to enhance the glory of his own sect, by such conduct inflicts the severest injury to his own sect." This ideal has been notably carried out in the world of Buddhism. As R. F. Johnston says, "Buddhism is perhaps the only great religion the world has known which not only teaches that the freedom of the human spirit is a desirable ideal, but achieves a more than moderate success in making its practice in this respect conform with its theory."[1]

Buddhism has never been arrogant or aggressive in its missionary work; all that its preachers claimed was the right to proclaim a new point of view. Wherever a differing faith prevailed they were well prepared to "accommodate" the local beliefs, and this tolerance has at times undoubtedly gone too far for the purity of Buddhism. But at least the spirit of accommodation is right, for it places the life of the Message before its forms, and is ever prepared to find new forms to express the evolving life. Hence the ethics of Thera Vâda, the philosophy and metaphysics of the Mahayana, and the ritual and magic of Tibet all find their place in the great field of Buddhism. There is therefore not only room in this for Zen, but room for limitless forms of Zen. For Buddhism cares not for the letter which killeth, but looks to the spirit which is life.

Already in the West the Hinayana, or Thera Vâda form of Buddhism has been studied and taught for fifty years; the Mahayana for nearly as long. Theosophy, established in London by H. P. Blavatsky in the 80s of last century, paved the way for the acceptance of principles common to both, and Zen has proved immensely popular among those who seek Reality beyond all forms. It may be that out of these various studies, at first kept separate by those who studied them, will come a western "yana" or vehicle for the Buddha's Enlightenment, a western Buddhism, by whatever name this new/old way of life may be known. The Thera Vâda purists would deplore such an event, and already evince their displeasure at the growing tendency. Buddhism, they say, is what they find in translations of the Pali Canon; all else is a lamentable

[1] *Buddhist China*, p. 330.

waste of time. The Mahayanists, who regard the Thera Vâda as already contained in the Mahayana, would approve; Zenthusiasts (I apologise—Zen enthusiasts) could not care less. All forms or yanas are to them but means or devices; all good, all equally bad.

Few doubt today that the West has need of a new enlightenment, which means that the old light, for the Light is one, is in need of a new expression. Our vaunted science changes its mind repeatedly, exchanging this month's final conclusions for those of the last; and its discoveries are handed over, with a gesture of washing the hands of all responsibility, to those whose ambition and livelihood is to kill their fellow men. Religion, too, has failed in the hour of adversity. Two world wars have struck such a blow at Christianity as may prove mortal; truth may be deathless, but its forms must die. It is just because Zen has no form which it is not willing on the least occasion to discard that it is immortal, for it is a wine that will use any bottle which comes in handy, or will make new bottles of its own. With the failure of Christianity, enquiring minds have sought new outlets for the religious sentiments of the mind. "Having lost the old faith, they turn eagerly to new ones, and science, psycho-analysis, spiritualism, social reform and nationalism have all in turn acted as substitutes for religion. Of these, nationalism has unfortunately proved to be the most successful. . . ."[1]

And the West is ripe for Buddhism in one form or another. As already indicated, the Theosophical Societies which, with thousands of individuals, together make up the Theosophical Movement, have for half a century taught the unity of life, Karma and rebirth, the impersonal approach to life and the universe, and many another principle which, as the two movements sprang from the same source, no genuine student of both will be surprised to find that they teach in common. And one psychologist at least has found the complementary background, an unconscious predilection for Buddhism, which readily explains its increasing popularity. As Graham Howe states, "Within ourselves we have our Eastern aspect, deeply buried, and yet still acting as our hidden source of light. In the course of their work many psychologists have found, as the pioneer work of C. G. Jung has shown, that we are all near-Buddhists on our hidden sides." He further explains how patients tend to produce what amounts to a common pattern of unconscious material, which has much in common with eastern

[1] *Diagnosis of Man*, KENNETH WALKER, p. 243.

art and philosophy. "To read a little Buddhism is to realise that the Buddhists knew, 2,500 years ago, far more about our modern problems of psychology than they have yet been given credit for. ... We are now rediscovering the ancient Wisdom of the East, and new knowledge is again coming from that direction as it has always done in the past."[1]

And as the process of satori seems to be an irruption of the unconscious content into the conscious mind, it may well be that the western unconscious, which already contains and seeks an outlet for this spiritual force, will welcome the opportunity.

But Alan Watts is possibly right when he says that Europeans test the value of a religion by the success which it achieves in bringing harmony into society as a whole, by its capacity to be reached and understood by "all sorts and conditions of men".[2] The East thinks differently.

It has no use for "mass religions", and knowledge is something sacred, to be handed by those who have earned it to those who may be trusted not to abuse it. Atomic energy should not be in the hands of the a-moral few, and in the East it would never be "revealed" save to those who would use it only in the service of mankind. As for social service, this is a result and not a cause; it is, or should be, the result of right thinking and, what is more rare and far more important, right understanding. At its best, and the phrase is coming to mean no more than political interference, it is the effect of a true religion or philosophy; it does not in itself supply that need.

What else does the West want? Something practical, that can be immediately applied to "usual life". Zen offers a "divination of the daily round", as it has been aptly described. It wants "a man's religion", for I agree with the late Dwight Goddard that the West is over-burdened with the other kind, "religions of authority and priest-craft, or ritual, and a faith that demands the setting aside of the individual mind, and the acceptance [of] and obedience to irrational dogmas and arbitrary authority". A man's religion, he says, must leave a man to do his own thinking and free to work out his own salvation in a way of his own choosing. "It must carry with it the lure of a great adventure. There must be no sham, no promise of quick and easy returns of magical healing and cheap emotion. It must not involve an unending expense, and it

---

[1] *Invisible Anatomy*, p. 5.
[2] *The Spirit of Zen*, p. 104.

must tend toward the support of the simple life. Such a man's religion is offered by Zen Buddhism."[1]

As for ritual, Aldous Huxley says that "ritual and ceremonial will arise almost spontaneously wherever masses of people are gathered together for the purpose of taking part in any activity in which they are emotionally concerned", and that "such rites and ceremonials will survive and develop for just so long as the emotional concern is felt. ... At the present time," he goes on, "the rites and ceremonies of traditional Christianity are at least demonstrably very ineffective, and have failed to stand up to the new god of nationalism."[2]

If all men tread the way of Jnana Yoga (Wisdom), or Bhakti Yoga (Devotion), or Karma Yoga (Action), then we English are Karma-Yogins. We express ourselves by what we do; we live in what we do; we are what we do. "Think of Zen, think of the Void, think of Good and Evil, and you are bound hand and foot. Think only and entirely and completely of what you are doing at the moment and you are as free as a bird."[3] Zen has no ritual, no prayer; no God that made us, nor a soul to be saved. All places are its temple and all things its altar furnishings. The desk and the work-bench and the sink are altars to the gods of Zen, and the first and only Commandment is, "Thou shalt walk on!"

The English have, and a few of them allow that other Europeans have, a great sense of humour. So has Zen. If humour is analysed (perish the thought!) much of it is found to be a revolt against logic; and the prevailing delight in "shaggy dog" stories, those which are pure nonsense and without any point at all, is surely a symptom of our weariness of the shackles of conceptual thought. If the intellect be so holy, so complete, why do intelligent people seek relief from it in nonsense? But if it be only partial, if in the jaws of its myriad opposites the mind grows weary, and longs, like a captive bird, to spread and use its wings, then men, whose intuition exists no less for its lack of conscious development, will at times grow restive. Like schoolboys who make fun of their masters behind their backs, they will laugh at the tyrant intellect, and equally at the fools who worship it.

One way, of course, of freeing the mind from the shackles of

---

[1] From an article: "Zen as a World Religion", in *Buddhism in England*, Vol. V. p. 116.

[2] *Ends and Means*, p. 229.

[3] BLYTH, p. 322.

thought is deliberate mind-development. All systems of meditation have much in common, and whether the method be that of the Society of Friends, that finest of all Christian sects who practise what they preach, or whether it be the Self-Communion of Raj-Yoga, is a question of means. The purpose is agreed, to free the mind from the fetters of self, which means the lower desire and the thought-machine. These means will vary with the student's temperament. The use of "self-power" (*jiriki*) or "other-power" (*tariki*) is a matter of technique. As explained in my *Via Tokyo*, the virtual Head of the Shin or Pure Land Sect of Japanese Buddhism agreed with me when I stated, in the presence of the Tariki pundits, that in the long view "self-power" and "other-power" were alike but means of self-enlightenment, for whether we coalesce the unconscious with the conscious (self-power) or pour the conscious into the unconscious (other-power) is, assuming that this is a fair description of the comparative process, a matter of temperament. Each method, self-abandonment to "God", or the growing awareness of "I and my Father are one", has its dangers, the former tending to the illusion that something or Someone really exists outside oneself with the power to save one, and the latter risking the spiritual vice of pride at having attained salvation, when in fact there is no self to attain it.

But whether the means of meditation be *jiriki* or *tariki*, Jnana, Bhakti or Karma Yoga, the West has need of the meditative habit, whether it be for a few minutes every day, for a whole day every month, for an annual "retreat" or, in the Zen way, for a habit of inward, poised attention each minute of the day. The steps of the ladder to satori are immaterial; the need for the unifying, or, as modern psychologists call it, the integrating experience is the same. "Though the mind of the eastern thinker may run to creative imagery, and that of the western worker to creative scientific achievement, yet the world into which they enter is curiously the same; the instrument of thought which they employ is called the 'mind' in the West and 'mind-stuff' in the East; both use the language of symbology to express their conclusions, and both reach the point where words prove futile to embody the intuited possibilities."[1] But when the eastern school breaks free alike from "creative imagery" and the "language of symbology" it is all the more free to create new forms for Zen.

As we know from Jung, some human beings are more introvert,

[1] *From Intellect to Intuition*, BAILEY, pp. 14–15.

others more extrovert, and the comparison equates, very vaguely, with East and West. But Zen is neither; it knows that whether one turns inward or outward one is the same. Both inner and outer are illusion; meanwhile here is a cup of tea, which is out, and my love of it, which is in, so why all these long words and furious distinctions? The glory is here, and now, and this; we need not look for it in the East or West.

> *"Not where the wheeling systems darken,*
> *And our benumbed conceiving soars!—*
> *The drift of pinions, would we hearken,*
> *Beats at our own clay-shuttered doors.*

> *"The angels keep their ancient places;*
> *Turn but a stone, and start a wing!*
> *'Tis ye, 'tis your estrangéd faces,*
> *That miss the many-splendoured thing."*[1]

Nor does the great antithesis between eastern and western modes of teaching stand in the way of Zen for the western mind. The East believes in the careful culture of the individual; the West, of the mass, while the individual exists but as part of the whole. Zen cares for neither and uses both. When there is but one, the individual and the mass, the culture of the individual is the mass, which gains thereby; the culture of the mass improves each individual. Yet in the end, "the race is run by one and one, and never by two and two," and it is the individual and never the mass which achieves Enlightenment.

A greater stumbling-block to the western mind's acceptance of Zen or, shall we say, to the awakening of Zen, which knows not East or West, in western minds, is the general belief, either consciously held or driven deep into the mind, in "God". In the western mind, which for 2,000 years has been rammed into the mould of Christian dogma, God is an "assumption" in every sense, philosophical, logical or psychological, of the term. He is assumed to exist, and from this unarguable premise all subsequent argument flows. When a western mind in fact breaks free from the dogma, either on learning that millions of his fellow men have never heard of it, and reject the conception when they do, or from a growing strength wherewith to face life as it is, there is a wonderful sense of freedom, as of a burden dropped or a fog that clears away. Of course there is, somewhere "behind" or "beyond" this unreal

---

[1] *In No Strange Land*, FRANCIS THOMPSON.

shadow world, an antithetical Reality, and it is not remarkable that men, immersed in the former, crave for the latter. Hence the great cry, to whatever gods may be, "From the unreal lead me to the Real ... from death to Immortality." But Zen points out that the unreal and the Real are alike unreal, for both are concepts of the mind. When hot, we crave for a cooling breeze; when cold, for the sun, but neither exists except in relation to the other. Samsara, the "Wheel of Becoming", and Nirvana, the end of it all, are one.

Granted that the average lazy man prefers to erect a God and then to petition it, with sacrifices of this and that, to do the work of "salvation" for him, but because men are lazy it does not follow that their efforts to avoid the work, either that of enlightening themselves, or of destroying the self which stands in the way of enlightenment by utterly dropping it (into the arms of God), will prove successful. The God may say, "Come unto me, all ye that are heavy laden," but those who begin the journey may find it a long and arduous road. And when they arrive? "Give us the core," said the small boy to his elder brother, who was eating an apple. "Core, core?" said the latter. "There ain't going to be no core!" What lies at the end of the road to God? I know not, but I firmly suspect that the answer is the summary already given of Zen's view of pantheism: "All is God—and there is no God!"

It is difficult to cleanse the mind of this conception, so comforting, so hoary with tradition. And the conception is psychologically the same whether God be completely personal, and lodged in the village tree, or ultra-refined into a glorious phrase like Parabrahman. Either it is THAT, and therefore not THIS, or it is so utterly THIS that there is no need to stretch the mind to include a hypothetical THAT. But the average believer in God, or user of the God-concept, wants the comfort which Someone, a mixture of Father at his best, the warmth of Love for a love-starved personality, and a kind of safety-net, such as hangs below the trapeze artist lest he miss his footing, so easily supplies. Remove the conception, and there is at first a yawning void and a feeling of frightening insecurity. Only when the first light of a Zen experience irradiates all consciousness is it perceived and KNOWN that the Void is filled—not only with the names of Love and Security and the like, but with the direct experience of their reality.

Zen, in brief, reduces the tension of all opposites, including the ultimate strain of THIS and THAT, by rising above them. When there is neither East nor West, who faces either?

The West needs integration, a making whole of a number of severed parts. Classes are riven in opposition; capital and labour, religion and daily life, the individual and the State contend; and these are symptoms of a dichotomy in the mind. The conscious and the unconscious wage their civil war, and none shall heal them. Zen alone, or the same experience under another name, can heal the mass neurosis and the individual ills. "Zen cannot help sufferers from organic spiritual disease, but it can help the spiritual neurotic who thinks himself spiritually incapacitated, or appears to be so to outsiders, but who in fact is only suffering from hyperfunction of his intellectual capacities, combined with infantile development of his intuition. This is specifically a disease of civilisation, and the vast majority of civilised persons may be correctly diagnosed as being too clever by half. The Kingdom is not to be entered by those who are possessed by their possessions. ..."[1] Alan Watts is right when he says that "Eastern doctrines are confessedly psychological rather than theological. Their intention is not to provide a satisfying explanation of the world and a theological sanction for morality; they exist simply to provide a technique for the soul's enlightenment."[2]

If religions are otherwise used they tend to become not aids but hindrances to spiritual growth. Jung has already been quoted on the subject. Even stronger is the famous Letter X in *The Mahatma Letters to A. P. Sinnett*, where the Master describes religion as "the chief cause of nearly two-thirds of the evils that pursue humanity ever since that cause became a power". It is all too easy to erect a scaffolding whereby to climb to the sun, and to end by making it a useless mountain of material which all but extinguishes the light.

Why, then, do notable minds consider that Zen will never be suitable to the West? We have seen good reason to the contrary; what is the ground of objection raised, and has it any validity?

In *The Meaning of Happiness* Alan Watts, who has studied the subject profoundly, says, if I may summarise, that it is unwise for a Westerner to become "converted" to an eastern religion, because in the West we have our own roots and traditions, our own dharma to fulfil. We must therefore distinguish between the acceptance of oriental religious principles, and their method of application. The former are universal; the latter particular to the East, and possibly

[1] W. J. GABB. From a MS.
[2] *The Legacy of Asia and Western Man*, p. 21.

inappropriate to the West. "We have to discover our own way of applying those principles. ..."[1] This, however, is not an objection to Zen in the West; only to a blind adoption of its peculiar technique. On what are the other objections based? They all seem to come back to some of Jung's remarks in *The Secret of the Golden Flower*, or those of his translator, the late Dr. Cary Baynes.

Dr. Baynes is obviously right in pointing out the dangers of the unintelligent adoption and imitation of eastern practices (p. vii). And none will doubt his summary: "Mastery of the inner world, with a relative contempt for the outer, must inevitably lead to great catastrophes. Mastery of the outer world, to the exclusion of the inner, delivers us over to the demonic forces of the latter and keeps us barbaric despite all outward forms of culture." Eastern spirituality and western science, he says, instead of deriding each other, must learn to walk hand in hand. But he passes, then, from the general to the particular. Have not the discoveries of modern science, he asks, for example that the world of so-called matter is really a world of energy, led him to look to the contents of his own mind as the source of that energy? In his view it is "the need of understanding himself in terms of change and renewal which most grips the imagination of modern man" (p. viii). But, as Jung himself points out, "If the wrong man uses the right means, the right means work in the wrong way" (p. 79). It is the man that matters, not the means. And in the end each man must develop himself. Instead of imitating the East he must remain true to himself, "and develop out of his own nature all that the East has brought forth from its inner being in the course of the centuries" (p. 82). In brief, "what the East has to give us should be merely a help in a work which we still have to do" (p. 146).

But how does this apply to Zen, which, I claim, is neither of the East nor West in spirit, and has no form? Strangely enough, the great intellect of Jung stops short at satori, like a bull that pauses at a gate. After reading Dr. Suzuki's *Introduction to Zen Buddhism*, he says, in writing the Foreword, "Satori depicts an art and a way of enlightenment which is practically impossible for the West to appreciate." But reading further, it is clear that the great man means no more than that he does not *understand* satori. Who does? Do not the Masters again and again point out that no one *understands* satori, and that he who tries to do so is robbing himself of the light which only circulates, to use the word of the

[1] Pp. 71–72.

Golden Flower, when all attempt to "understand" is finally abandoned?

In brief, Zen is to be used, not sought, or described or understood. It has no clothes, no body. Why, then, should it feel ashamed in a collar and trousers? Or in a jumper and skirt? Zen votes for direct action; the West is moving towards it in many ways. Children are taught to swim by being dropped in the water; they soon learn. They are taught the piano by being placed in front of it and encouraged to make a noise; to draw by trying to draw, to speak some foreign language by speaking the words they know and with them learning more. All this is Zen, to do it and not merely to talk about it, to experience life, "good", "bad" and indifferent, and to ignore these man-made labels. Jiu-jitsu is already here, and for thirty years that remarkable figure, Mr. G. Koizumi, has spread through Europe a knowledge of Judo technique and, what is more important, by Judo practice something of the Zen of which it is the finest physical expression. For here again one learns to throw a man by throwing him, not by text-books, sermons, or sound advice.

And the medium for this knowledge? The Buddhist Society, London, has for twenty years made known the principles of Zen. For a year or more a Zen class has met at the Society's premises, and if we lack a Zen Master, we find that a strenuous-minded audience, bent on achieving satori as distinct from information about it, can use to a promising extent the *mondo* and *innen* technique. At the least the bonds of the intellect are progressively loosened, and the light of the intuition grows. There is more natural laughter and less "earnestness", more positive tension of will with less of the mental strain which kills achievement. And the effect on those who attend is at least the birth of the qualities which flower in satori. In brief, I believe that Zen, intelligently handled, has a part to play in the future of the West. The size of that part depends on the number of those who achieve some measure of satori; the depth of that achievement depends on the skill of those who find the Absolute Moment in assisting others to the same awareness, that certain, sweet serenity of Zen.

Chapter 12

Let's try it!

But we are still talking about Zen, and even murdering it by discussing whether or not it is "suitable" here or there. For Zen, like Tao, only exists in use.

> *"When one looks at it, one cannot see it;*
> *When one listens to it, one cannot hear it.*
> *However, when one uses it, it is inexhaustible."*[1]

"Anything not based upon experience is outside Zen," says Dr. Suzuki. Let us, therefore, use Zen. The man in front of me in the street drops his umbrella. I pick it up and give it to him. He smiles and thanks me. We both walk on. Well? I did not think what to do or feel emotional about it. I just did it, or, as in the exercise on self-control of the Southern School of Buddhism, "there was a doing" of the act, for the "I" for once was silent. But why not run the whole of life this way? There is a friend in need; let there be a helping of him. There is no need to worry about him, or even to think about his woes; just do what you can and walk on. There is a washing-up to be finished, or a war to be won; let them be done. Keep the emotions where they belong, for they have no part in "right" action, and none at all in thought. But do not repress them. If yours is an emotional temperament, use them, develop them, express the highest in you by their means. And if it is not, do not ignore them. Take them for a run at times. Sing, shout, get excited, whether with great beauty, a local football match or, best of all, great fun. Compete, if you will, in sport or trade or politics, so long as you do not imagine that it matters in the least who wins. It is the excitement itself, the letting off steam, which matters; the game, whether of football, national politics or international war, has no intrinsic validity. There is only Mind—Mind-Only; the rest is the crackling of thorns under a pot.

All this is using Zen, for Zen is life, and all life, whether that of the film-star or the maggot, is good Zen. But let us apply it to more

[1] *Tao Te Ching*, Chap. XXXV.

serious things, if there are more serious things, which , as we say in the Law, is not admitted. How do you solve a problem? The answer should be that you don't. If you are wise you never allow it to be born. "All difficult things in the world start from the easy; all great things in the world start from the small." Thus the *Tao Te Ching*. And again, better still, "Deal with a thing before it comes into existence." There lies the solution, for the problem, do not forget, is born in, and has its sole existence in, the mind. It is raining and you have left your umbrella behind. That is not in itself a problem. Nor is the fact that you are in debt, have lost your job, and are being pressed to pay. These facts in a relative world are relatively true, but the problem is something added to the facts by your mind. You must either, therefore, kill it at birth, or later "solve" it, remembering that the larger it grows the larger will be the Giant which Jack the Giant-Killer will have to kill. But even if it is allowed to arise, do not attempt to solve it; dissolve it. For you and the problem are not two things in opposition but one thing; you are One, though still two, in Jijimuge. You are the problem and the problem is you. Where, then, is the problem? When the puppy and kitten fight on the hearth-rug you look down on them with serene, amused indifference. Do the same with problems of health and wealth and home and family. Get up; look up, and then look down at the hearth-rug. Where is now the problem which you so foolishly made?

The Zen way of getting the goose out of the bottle is, as we have seen, to appreciate the fact that it is already out. W. J. Gabb has applied this to western psychology. "Zen, as I understand it, use it and love it, is the address of the whole of my being to the circumstances of the particular situation in which I find myself. It is Zen itself that draws me forth, and Zen itself responds."[1] Use Zen as the mathematician uses the symbol for infinity. He does not solve the symbol, but he uses it to solve all else.

It must by now be clear that we do not solve any problem on its own plane. How can we? The relationship between two things is a higher third. Rise to the plane where the distinction disappears and, the poles of the problem having vanished, there is nothing left to be solved. For a problem implies tension, a tearing of the self in two. But if the self be felt as one untearable whole, where is the tension between this part of it and that; where is the problem? In one sense the problem is never faced as such, for the life-strength,

[1] From an unpublished MS.

the flow of the river of life within you, is concentrated on a plane where the shrill, complaining cry of the opposites is no longer heard. When you do not care whether you are wet or dry, there is no problem in finding yourself on a rainy day without an umbrella. And when you no longer care whether or not the local bicycle club or the British Empire dissolves by reason of your absence from its deliberations, there remains no problem in the only place in which it ever existed, your own mind. If you attend, you attend; if you don't, you don't, but why worry about it?

Lift, lift your mind, your portion of All-Mind, as high as you can. A spark of the Universal Mind will sooner or later flash between the terminals of each and every problem, and burn them out of existence. Therefore see to it that the self is, if not dead, at least no longer rampant, for the more there is to be burnt the more painful the burning, and the higher forces of the Unconscious are not to be ignored.

Leave all problems unsolved, says Mr. Gabb, and supply the answer. Address the situation from the highest within you and apply the response. Leave the intellect to fight its own fights in the boxing ring, even though it spends as much energy in hitting the air as it does in hitting its opponent. As for you, stop thinking. All problems are thought into existence; drop them. "A single thought and you separate yourself from reality. All empirical thought is vain, for you cannot use the mind to seek something from mind."[1] And this means all thought. "Let the difference be even the tenth of an inch, and heaven and earth are set apart," said a Zen Master. One single concept and the world of non-discrimination, of satori, is hurled to earth.

Just accept the problem and its possible implications; take it, if need be, on the jaw. If possible, take it the Judo way, by gently stepping aside so that the problem, when it strives to engulf you, finds that you have just moved out of the way. But it is dangerous to personify one's enemies, for it leads one to forget that they only exist in the mind. The Taoist doctrine of *wu-wei* is excellent Zen. Non-action, as it is often translated, does not mean no action, but no such action as begets opposition. "Right" action is neither to oppose nor to give way, but to be pliable, as a reed in the wind. In the West we are too pugnacious, so quick to fight all circumstance that we make by our very violence more problems than exist to be solved. It is wiser to walk delicately, "with a hold on life so light

[1] *The Huang Po Doctrine*, p. 29.

that it would not ruffle the bloom on a butterfly's wing". Serene, detached from all results, ready to fight or run, to win or lose, and always ready to laugh at all things, take whatever comes. Your child is ill, you say, or you cannot pay the rent. Very well, accept these facts and face them. Are they not trouble enough in themselves without adding the aggravation of worry to them? Why add the tension of emotion-thought to a situation which is (a) illusion, (b) to the extent that it is real, of passing moment, and (c) in any event the result of previous causes? Do what seems wise to be done, forget it and walk on. Even if you come to a precipice, why walk round it or back from it? Why not go over it? It is probably the shortest way there!

Acceptance can, of course, be unpleasant, but just as you alone make the problem so do you add the label "unpleasant" to an experience which is neither pleasant nor unpleasant, but that experience. If you cannot pay your debts without selling the house, sell it. If you have no umbrella in the rain, get wet. Does it matter? All things, your house and your umbrella included, have no validity outside your mind, and even your body will go in a few years, or perhaps tomorrow. All problems, even of the twin illusions of life and death, are alike good fun, if so regarded. Was any man ever the happier for being unhappy about death, and did he live any longer? Is suffering made the less by tears about it? Or another's pain removed by your abundant gloom?

Is all this unintelligible? Then try it, for only so will its worth be known, and it is the key to the "unemotional" approach to life of the Zen student, and his habitual happiness. "I can't make head or tail of it," a friend complained. Why try to make head or tail of it? Zen has no head or tail, and looks the same whether upside down or downside up. Is it unbelievable? Learn to accept the unbelievable as facts, for life is neither believable nor rational. It just is. The White Queen in *Alice Through the Looking-Glass* actually practised believing the impossible. Sometimes, she claimed, she believed as many as six impossible things before breakfast. How much wiser she was than many a modern scientist who, failing to understand some natural law, refuses to believe in it. I do not know the nature of electricity (nor, for that matter, does any scientist) but I use it, and thus believe in it.

And the technique of it all? Start from the middle instead of making the middle the goal. Begin with enlightenment, and all things will be added unto you. "The Chinese author," says Dr.

Jung, "always starts from the centre of things, from the point we would call his objective goal; in a word, he begins with the ultimate insight he has set out to attain."[1] First gain satori—"There! It's out!"—then look back at the goose and the bottle.

But this is not an armchair job. To raise a car above your head is child's play compared with raising your consciousness one inch. "Nature," it has been said, "spews the lukewarm from her mouth," and there is nothing lukewarm in Zen. The will is the man, and Zen appeals to it. Life may be a Wheel of Becoming, a chain of causation. Leap from the Wheel, break the chain; take manifestation in your two bare hands and make of it what you will. Strangely enough, manifestation will be delighted to find such a real Man in the many-millioned rabbit-farm we call the world. The Kingdom of Heaven is taken by storm, even though the great strength which returns the penny is an artful letting go, an acceptance of all things for what they are. In any event, be utterly whole-hearted. Make Zen your work and play, your love, your hate, your everything. Said D. H. Lawrence:

> "There is no point in work
> unless it absorbs you
> like an absorbing game.
>
> "If it doesn't absorb you,
> if it's never any fun,
> don't do it."

The same applies to Zen. Adopt it, live it, love it, become it; let it flow through the veins as cosmic fire, caring not what it is, nor whence it comes, but using it with every breath and offering it again to the world. Is all this cold, unlit with the light of love which radiates on the wave-length of compassion to all forms of life? Listen again to the famous Four Great Vows which the monks of Engakuji, for example, the Zen monastery where Dr. Suzuki himself resides, recite at the end of every lecture by the spiritual Head of the monastery.

> "How innumerable sentient beings are, I vow to save
> them all;
> How inexhaustible our evil passions are, I vow to
> exterminate them;

[1] The Secret of the Golden Flower, p. 94.

> How immeasurable the holy doctrines are, I vow to
> study them;
> How inaccessible the path to Buddha is, I vow to
> attain it."

Is that not enough for one life's work, or even for a dozen lives to come?

Instead of conclusion

Let us summarise. Life is flow and Zen is the flow of it. It is therefore neither Buddhism nor any other "ism"; it was not born neither will it die. Now we develop, according to Indian philosophy, from *Tamas*, Inertia, a cabbage life of thinking, feeling and doing the minimum, enwrapped in sloth (ignorance, *avidyâ*), through *Rajas* to *Sattva*. *Rajas* is activity, desire for activity, the libido or *élan vital* functioning through the self-ness of the average individual. It is effort, personal ambition; hence competition and consequent war. By means of *Rajas*, however, we develop energy, "horse-power", will-power, "guts". We begin to move, albeit for selfish purposes. But this will is colourless; it is the horse-power of the car and not its driver. But, "Behind will stands desire". Desire is of the self, self-ish, and at first the self is just "I", the "I" of the egotist and the utterly self-ish man. Then the self, in the guiding reins and blinkers of morality, grows from this personal "I" to family, from family to tribe and nation and finally, via all mankind, to all creation. The false self fades to nothing; the true Self grows to all.

In the later stages of morality comes *bhavana*, the development of the mind. The mind learns to refuse to react to bodily impulses, to be clouded by emotion. It learns to see, to understand, though still by the cumbersome and second-hand method of rationalisation, the process of conceptual thought. It is not above the sway of the opposites. It still believes that by their use a thing called Science and a thing called Philosophy can lead the heart to the outer and inner aspects of a thing called Truth. Meanwhile, it leaves the emotions in a local crèche called Religion where they cannot interrupt the pursuits of their elders and betters.

But the intellect is found in time to be strictly finite, to be limited in its approach to Truth, to fail to go all the way. It teaches about Truth or about some part of it—(is not an expert one who learns more and more about less and less?). It cannot merge the Known and the Unknown in one, much less achieve the ultimate relationship of Jijimuge.

What then? In his struggles to perfect the intellectual instrument, the student further develops its horse-power, and carries the process further still when the intellect begins to butt its head against the ceiling of its intellectual cage. The tension grows. The will, driven by desire for Truth, begins to destroy the limitations of its instrument. If intellect, shackled by the opposites, limps on the windy heights of self-becoming, new means of ascent must be developed and used. It need not be found, for it is all there, waiting, a complete outfit ready for development and use. Some seekers develop it consciously; some, stretching the thought-machine to its limits, so break up the roof that the sun of Awareness increasingly breaks in. Sooner or later some means or technique is adopted to speed the process. "Prayer," "Meditation," the Zen koan, all in their higher methods achieve the same end. All, at some stage or, to be more accurate, at frequently recurring stages of progress and cyclic expansion, lead to the same precipice, the same bold, exciting jump and the same safe landing in *Sattva*, the serene and certain joy which is known in Zen as satori.

But satori comes slowly, I believe, and differently for different seekers according to their present mental makeup, and, what is really the same thing, their Karma, both in this life and in lives gone by. If one may generalise from known material, the process is, at least frequently, as follows:

At first the higher state of awareness illumines higher thought. The light of satori brightens the upper levels of the intellect. One may suddenly have a "bright idea" about life or even a business problem—a flash of clear perception, so brilliant and simple that you cannot understand why you did not "see" it before. Then, or concurrently, come brief flashes of insight at a much higher level. Then come, or it may be that they have already come, longer periods of a lower level of satori when the normal consciousness knows that it is enjoying this higher state of awareness. Then, especially if meditation of some kind is regularly practised, some level of satori, though at first a low one, is attainable, if not at will, at least in the more successful sessions of inward-turned attention. In the Pali Canon we read of the *Jhanas* (Sanskrit, *Dhyâna*) which the late Mrs. Rhys Davids would call "musings", but which are surely far higher than the ordinary meaning of that term. Rather are they a raising of consciousness to successively higher levels of Awareness from the *rupa*, or form worlds, however fine the form, to the *arupa*, formless planes of ever purer abstraction. This stage develops into the power of achieving this state of consciousness anywhere at any time, like the turning on of a switch, even though the effort to do so be considerable. It is like heaving oneself out of the mud to stand on a rock to touch the sky. The "squulch" of the extraction is almost audible. Thereafter all processes proceed together, the height, duration and control of the Satori experience depending, of course, on the aspirant.

Is all this difficult? Of course; what worth the doing is not? But as the Master K. H. said to his pupil, A. P. Sinnett, "We have one word for all aspirants—TRY."[1]

The rewards, as already described, are commensurate. Satori, at any level, brings serenity. Above the tension of the opposites, above the turmoil of emotion which, creating nothing, clouds the mirror of the mind; beyond, if not desire, at least the more personal desires, even the lower levels of satori give "Such a peace I did not hope to find this side of heaven".

Satori brings certainty. Where there are no opposites there is no need to choose between them. The captain on the bridge, now more or less captain of his soul, is no longer at the orders of his servant bodies; even the intellect is now an instrument. There is an understanding that all is somehow "right", a sense of flowing with the rhythm of things. Patience comes of itself when time is seen as a convenient illusion in which all things moving on the Wheel of birth, growth, decay and death, are alike illusion, and tolerance comes with an understanding of the innumerable paths by which men climb (albeit bumping into each other on the way) to the mountain top. And as every "thing" is right and my own action (so long as "I" do not interfere with it) is also right, my part in the general rightness of things is a vision of actuality and not a mere sentimental dream. This sounds admittedly like the drunkard's "certainty". "S'all right ol' man; everything s'all right." Well, perhaps there is an element of spiritual inebriety in the "divine afflatus". One certainly sings for joy.

There is a sense of Now and Here and This, which is the heart of Zen. Wherever I go I am here, for I cannot go anywhere else. Wherever I move my conscience in time, it is now. Whatever I handle or hold, it is this. "There" becomes "here" when I get there. "Then" becomes "now" when it is. "That" becomes "this" when I look at it. There is neither divine nor human, holy nor profane. Have you seen the huge metal sports-wheel, for use on a beach or lawn, like a magnified stand for a garden hose in which the player in a bathing dress stands with feet and hands gripping the inside of the outer frame and makes it revolve with muscle effort of alternate

---

[1] *Mahatma Letters to A. P. Sinnett* (second edition), p. 247.

pushing and pulling (the opposites in full play)? When the wheel is in motion there is neither up nor down; head (spirit) and feet (of clay) are alternately on top—for both are one in motion (life). And how does it begin to move? By deliberately turning oneself upside down with vaunted head below and despised feet in the sky. Verb.sap.!

I have now written over 50,000 words on Zen and have said less than Gerald Gould has said in a line and a half of poetry, when he speaks of "A careless trust in the divine occasion of our dust".

Read that again. Can the late author have realised the world-philosophy which he packed into ten English words? The satori lies in "careless". The rest is merely genius.

Satori means selflessness, which is neither being a prig nor a bore. It is a realisation that "man stands in his own light and wonders why it is dark". The Self has taken over, and the appetites of a pack of assorted ill-trained animals which yelp and growl and bite at each other, and do far ruder things than that, have at least been recognised as such. If they do slip off the new lead sometimes, it is at least with the master's knowledge, if not with his consent.

Thereafter the master, if not yet worthy of that title in the vast fraternity of "men made perfect", is at least worthy to tread that Path of occult Wisdom which leads to adeptship. When a man is master of life and death, "there is no more going out". Such a one might say, though he would not say it, in the words of a famous Japanese set of verses,

"*I have no parents; I make heaven and earth my parents.*
I have no means; I make docility my means.
I have neither life nor death; I make AUM my life and death.
I have no body; I make stoicism my body.
I have no limbs; I make promptitude my limbs.
I have no design; I make opportunity my design.
I have no principle; I make adaptability to all things my principle.
I have no friends; I make my mind my friend.
I have no enemy; I make incautiousness my enemy.
I have no armour; I make good will and righteousness my armour.
I have no castle; I make immovable mind my castle.
I have no sword. I make the sleep of the mind my sword."[1]

And the sleep of the mind is Zen.

[1] Adapted from the version in MRS. ADAMS BECK'S *Garden of Vision*, p. 331.

But how does one begin to develop the intuition? The answer *should* be obvious. There should be a dozen books on the subject but I know of none. Therefore, lest it be said that this brief study of Zen is not practical, let me add in all humility a brief ladder which has led me, and seems to be leading others, to a land of such "careless" sunlight, song and joy as only the "few" from the Battle of Self may know.

THE DEVELOPMENT OF INTUITION

Preliminary exercises

(a) *Laugh*. Roar with laughter. There is nothing, no single thing in this whole vast Universe worth taking as seriously as you at present are taking yourself.

(b) *Be serious*. Deadly serious. There is nothing, no single thing in the whole vast Universe more enormously important than lighting your pipe or powdering your nose or washing up. Your Saturday night outing and your Sunday morning prayer-meeting are both tremendously and equally important/unimportant.

(c) *Undress*. Take off these diver's boots of belief in God, soul, divine and not-quite-nice. Take off the suits and frocks of conventional beliefs and social rules and prejudices about everything under the sun, from the way to grow roses to the International Problem of East and West. Both will get on very nicely without your help. Now take off your "undies" of personal private convictions and ideals. Now blush. There isn't much left, is there?

Now we will begin.

(1) *Form the habit of synthesis of thought*. Most of our time is spent in analysing differences. Now concentrate on similarities, on what is common between two things which are habitually regarded as antagonistic opposites. In other words, look for the higher thirds above all opposites, for in fact there is no such thing as two. There is one or three, for all things are only visible in the light of their relationship. Look for this relationship, and you will be kinder to each of the pairs. This exercise involves, of course, the study of the opposite bank of the river. If you are young, study the older generation's point of view, and see its value; if you are male, study the female point of view. It is quite as good as yours. Don't judge until you have heard and seen the value of both sides. Then judge, not between them or even above them, but within them, and

you will see that, like the two sides of the penny, they are one.

(2) *Learn to objectivise*. Face your circumstances such as home, office conditions, family affairs, hobbies and fancies, all of which are physical. Face your love affairs or great hopes and fears, all of which are emotional. Then do the same with your mind. Write down, if you will, your convictions and ideals, your beliefs and religious principles. Look at them, examine them; are they true? Feel them, focus upon them and wait. You are now looking at your intellect—with something else; let it speak. Are you now so certain that *this* is true and *that* worth living for?

(3) *Meditate*. This focus of all attention on an object (which, by the intensity of concentration, becomes subject) is best achieved in meditation. Therefore meditate at least for a few minutes every day; it matters not when, where or how. Learn the value of silence, of being alone with the best of you. Let the silence speak to you, not with ideas (about it and about) but with a bright and gentle certainty. Learn to listen.

(4) *Encourage the intuitive factor in the mind*. Look for it, believe in it, trust it, use it. Don't hit it on the head when it speaks and say, "That's nonsense, I can't do that!" It may be nonsense; it may none the less be true. Don't fritter away your attention in gossip, "news"-papers, empty films. They are not "wrong" and still less "sin", for there are no such things. They are, however, a waste of time, and in the noise of the market place a whisper of truth is not easily heard.

Yet check this whisper with your reason. Much that passes for intuition is only physical instinct or prejudice dressed up, or promptings from the psychic plane, and the psychic is just three planes removed from the intuition. Meanwhile, while waiting for satori itself, induce the results of it. Lift yourself up to a plane of certainty, sincerity, impersonal rightness of action and a sense of the flow of the Universe. Boldly feel yourself an active agent of All-Power, All-Life, but see to it that you are an impersonal agent, for self, the personal, self-seeking self at the wrong end of the cosmic wave-length gets rudely knocked about.

(5) *Expand your understanding till it hurts*. Take in more and more. Expand in time, with the knowledge of hundreds of millions of years, of light years, to the nearest star. Then move through space from earth to the sun, and thence from solar system to solar system till the brain reels and the very stars go wheeling round the sky.

Expand the opposites to ultimates of time and space, of ultimate form and ultimate life itself. .... Now come back with a bump to your neighbour's faults about which you have so long and bitterly complained. Can you not understand his "sin", his crime, his foolishness, you that are so tolerant of your own? Can you not see the muddled wants and hopes and fears within his mind, and the consequent foolish actions of this fellow infinitesimal speck of the infinite All-mind?

(6) *Stop rushing about*. You are always here and it is always now and you are always concerned with this. "Be still and know that I am God." Who is? This, here and now; there is no other, within or without the Universe. Learn to feel "the divine occasion of our dust". Waste nothing, not even the dust. Aim at the "right" use of everything.

(7) *Relax*. Don't strain, for nothing is worth the while. There is nothing to be found, so why this effort to find it? Sit loose to life, for it flows about you, and if you are wise, you are happily flowing too. Just drop it, whatever it is that is worrying you, and go on dropping it. Laugh and laugh still more; if you cannot, find out why.

(8) *Walk on!*

Such is a book about Zen. Of the truth which is Zen and even of the occult arts and sciences which remain unwritten in the hands of the Masters of Zen, it may be repeated, "He who knows, does not speak; he who speaks does not know."

Light your own lamp.

Abbreviations used in footnotes

(For further details of works see Bibliography)

BLYTH. *Zen in English Literature and Oriental Classics*, R. H. Blyth.

BUDDHISM IN ENGLAND. *The Journal of the Buddhist Society*, London. Now *The Middle Way*.

BUDDHA AND GOSPEL. *The Buddha and the Gospel of Buddhism*, Coomaraswamy.

ESSAYS I.
ESSAYS II. } *Essays in Zen Buddhism*, Series I, II and III, D. T. Suzuki.
ESSAYS III.

GABB. The MS. of a book provisionally entitled *Studies in Zen Buddhism*, being lectures on Zen together with previous booklets, *Beyond the Intellect*, and *Tales of Tokuzan*. Published by the Buddhist Society 1956 as *The Goose is Out*.

HUANG PO. *The Huang Po Doctrine of Universal Mind*. Translated Chu Ch'an.

INTRODUCTION. *An Introduction to Zen Buddhism*, D. T. Suzuki (first edition). *Note*: References to C. G. Jung's Foreword to the second edition, are to the second edition, and are so marked in the footnotes.

McGOVERN INTRODUCTION. *Introduction to Mahayana Buddhism*, William McGovern.

PRATT. *The Pilgrimage of Buddhism and a Buddhist Pilgrimage*, J. B. Pratt.

WEI LANG. *The Sutra of Wei Lang*. New edition by Christmas Humphreys.

ZEN BUDDHISM AND INFLUENCE. *Zen Buddhism and Its Influence on Japanese Culture*, Suzuki.

Bibliography of works consulted

A   Books and Booklets on Zen.
B   Scriptures, and Commentaries on Scriptures used in Zen.
C   Books containing chapters or sections on Zen.
D   Articles on Zen.
E   Books containing Cognate Material.
F   Unpublished Manuscripts.
G   Zen in Fiction.
H   Further Works on Zen.

A.   Books and Booklets on Zen

BLYTH, R. H. *Zen in English Literature and Oriental Classics*, 1942.
DUMONLIN. H. and SASAKI, R. F. *The Development of Chinese Zen*, 1953.
GABB, W. J. *Beyond the Intellect; Tales of Tokuzan*, 1944. Reprinted as *The Goose is Out* 1956.
HERRIGEL, E. *Zen in the Art of Archery*, 1953.
KAITEN NUKARIYA, *The Religion of the Samurai*, 1913.
OGATA, SOHAKU. *A Guide to Zen Practice*, 1934.
SENZAKI, N. AND M. CANDLESS, R.S. *Buddhism and Zen*, 1953.
SOYEN SHAKU. *Sermons of a Buddhist Abbot*, 1906.
SUZUKI, D. T. *Essays in Zen Buddhism*, first series, 1927; second series, 1933; third series, 1934; *An Introduction to Zen Buddhism*, 1934; *The Training of the Zen Buddhist Monk*, 1934; *Manual of Zen Buddhism*, 1935; *Buddhist Philosophy and its Effects on the Life and Thought of the Japanese People* (Kokusai Bunka Shinkokai), 1936; *Buddhism in the Life and Thought of Japan*, 1937; *Zen Buddhism and its Influence on Japanese Culture*, 1938; *Japanese Buddhism* (Tourist Library Series No. 21), 1938; *The Essence of Buddhism* (second edition), 1947; *Studies in Zen*. 1955.
WALEY. ARTHUR. *Zen Buddhism and its Relation to Art*, 1922.
WATTS. ALAN. *The Spirit of Zen* (Wisdom of the East Series), 1936; *Zen Buddhism—A New Outline and Introduction*, 1947 (this is a re-written edition of this author's *Outline of Zen Buddhism*, 1932).

B.   Scriptures and Commentaries on Scriptures used in Zen

A Catena of Scriptures from the Chinese. Beal, 1871.
The Diamond Sutra. Trans. Gemmell, 1912.
The Jewel of Transcendental Wisdom (The Diamond Sutra). Trans. A. F. Price, 1947.
The Lankâvatâra Sutra. Trans. D. T. Suzuki, 1932.
The Huang Po Doctrine of Universal Mind. Trans. Chu Ch'an, 1947.
The Path to Sudden Attainment. Trans. John Blofeld, 1948.
The Sutra of Wei Lang (Hui-neng). New edition by Christmas Humphreys, 1944.
The Sutra of 42 Sections, and two other Scriptures of the Mahayana School. Trans. Chu Ch'an, 1947.

The Teaching of Buddha. A compendium of many scriptures trans. from the Japanese. The Federation of All Young Buddhist Associations of Japan, 1934. (American edition by Dwight Goddard, published as *Buddha, Truth and Brotherhood*, 1934.)

Ten Bulls of Zen. Trans. Senzaki and Reps, 1935.

The Gateless Gate (The Mumon-kwan). Trans. Senzaki and Reps, 1934.

101 Zen Stories. Trans. Senzaki and Reps, 1940.

C.   Books containing Chapters or Sections on Zen

ANESAKI. *Buddhist Art* (A History of Japanese Religion), 1916.

ARMSTRONG, R. C. *Buddhism and Buddhists in Japan*, 1927.

BECK, MRS. ADAMS. *The Story of Oriental Philosophy*, 1928.

BLOFELD, JOHN. *The Jewel in the Lotus*, 1948.

COOMARASWAMY, ANANDA. *The Buddha and the Gospel of Buddhism*, 1916.

HARRISON, E. J. *The Fighting Spirit of Japan*, 1913.

HUMPHREYS, CHRISTMAS. *What is Buddhism? An Enquiry from the Western Point of View*, 1928; *Concentration and Meditation*, 1935; *Studies in the Middle Way*, 1940.

JOHNSTON, R. F. *Buddhist China*, 1913.

KEYSERLING, COUNT. *The Travel Diary of a Philosopher*, 2 vols., 1925.

OKAKURA KAKUZO. *The Book of Tea*, 1919.

PRATT, J. B. *The Pilgrimage of Buddhism and a Buddhist Pilgrimage*, 1928.

SANSOM, G. B. *Japan.*

SUZUKI, D. T. *Philosophy—East and West*, edited Moore; Chapter, *An Interpretation of Zen Experience*, 1944.

TAKAKUSU. *The Essentials of Buddhist Philosophy*, 1947.

D.   Articles on Zen

BLYTH, R. H. "Zen and Haiku." *The Cultural East*, Vol. I, p. 7 and later issues.

GABB, W. J. "Infinite Regress in the Light of Zen Buddhism." *Buddhism in England*, Vol 14, p. 38.

GODDARD, DWIGHT. "Zen as a World Religion." *Buddhism in England*, Vol. 5, p. 114.

HOWE, DR. E. GRAHAM. "The Creative Relation." *The Middle Way*, Vol. 23, p. 85.

HUMPHREYS, CHRISTMAS. "Buddhism in Modern Europe." *The Aryan Path*, Vol. 16, p. 375.

OGATA, THE VEN SOHAKU. "The Zen Way of Life." *Buddhism in England*, Vol. II, p. 176; "Zen for the West," *Ibid*, Vol. 12, p. 104.

SALANAVE, MRS. MURIEL. "The Excellent Path." *Buddhism in England*, Vol. 7, pp. 110, 153 and 185.

SASAKI, MRS. RUTH. "A Zen Student's Experience and Advice." *Buddhism in England*, Vol. 8, pp. 13 and 48.

SIREN, DR. OSVALD. "Ch'an (Zen) Buddhism and its Relation to Art." *The Theosophical Path*, October, 1934.

SUZUKI, MRS. B. L. "Zen Meditation." *Buddhism in England*, Vol. 7, p. 42; "Zen at Engakuji." *Ibid*, p. 50.

SUZUKI, PROF. D. T. Numerous articles in *The Eastern Buddhist*, published in Japan, 1921–1939; "The Message of Bodhidharma." *The Aryan Path*, January,

1936; "The Zen Sect of Buddhism." *The Journal of the Pali Text Society*, 1906–1907, reprinted as a pamphlet, 1907; "Tea-Room Meditations." *The Cultural East*, Vol. I, p. 29; "The Swordsman and the Cat" (translated). *The Cultural East*, Vol. I, No. 2, p. 37; "Zen and Japanese Art." *Bulletin of Eastern Art*, No. 37, p. 1 (1943); "The Threefold Question in Zen." *The Middle Way*, Vol. 23, p. 52.

E. *Books Containing Cognate Material*

BAILEY, ALICE. *From Intellect to Intuition.*
BINYON, LAURENCE. *The Flight of the Dragon; The Spirit of Man in Asian Art.*
BLAVATSKY, H. P. *The Secret Doctrine.*
BUCKE, R. M. *Cosmic Consiousness.*
CRANMER-BYNG, L. *The Vision of Asia.*
EDKINS, JOSEPH. *Chinese Buddhism.*
GATENBY, E. V. *The Cloud Men of Yamato.*
GILES, H. A. *Chuang Tzu.*
GROUSSET, RÉNÉ. *In the Footsteps of the Buddha.*
HUMPHREYS, CHRISTMAS. *Walk On!*
HUGHES, E. R. *China's Philosophy in Classical Times.*
HUXLEY, ALDOUS. *Ends and Means; The Perennial Philosophy.*
HOWE, E. GRAHAM. *The Triumphant Spirit; Invisible Anatomy.*
JAMES, WILLIAM. *The Varieties of Religious Experience.*
JUNG, CARL. *Psychology and Religion; Essays on Contemporary Events;* (with Wilhelm). *The Secret of the Golden Flower.*
KIMURA, R. K. *Historical Study of the Terms Hinayana and Mahayana.*
MASON, J. W. G. *The Creative East.*
NOGUCHI, YONE. *The Spirit of Japanese Poetry.*
RADHAKRISHNAN, PROFESSOR S. *Eastern Religion and Western Thought.*
SAUNDERS, KENNETH. *The Pageant of Asia.*
UNDERHILL, EVELYN. *Practical Mysticism.*
WALKER, KENNETH. *Diagnosis of Man.*
WATTS, ALAN. *The Legacy of Asia; The Meaning of Happiness.*
YAMAKUNI, SOGEN. *Systems of Buddhistic Thought.*

F. *Unpublished Manuscripts*

Living by Zen. D. T. Suzuki. [Published 1950].
The Zen Doctrine of No-Mind. D. T. Suzuki. [Published 1949].
Studies in Zen Buddhism. W. J. Gabb. [Published as *The Goose is Out* in 1956].

G. *Zen in Fiction*

The Garden of Vision. Mrs. Adams Beck. Many other stories by the same writer in such works as *The Perfume of the Rainbow,* and *Dreams and Delights.*

H. *Further Works on Zen*

BENOIT, HUBERT. *The Supreme Doctrine.* Trans. from French, 1955.
BLOFELD, JOHN. *The Zen Teaching of Huang Po* (Revised translation), 1958; *The Zen Teaching of Hui Hai,* 1962.

BLYTH, R. H. *Zen and Zen Classics*. Volume One Includes Commentary on the Hsinhsinming, 1960; Volume Four. His Commentary on the Mumonkan, 1966.

CHANG, CHEN-CHI. *The Practice of Zen*, 1959.

CHANG, CHUNG-YUAN. *Original Teachings of Zen Buddhism*, 1969.

DUMOULIN, HEINRICH, S.J. *The History of Zen Buddhism*. Trans. from German, 1963.

HARDING, DOUGLAS. *On having no Head*, 1961.

HUMPHREYS, CHRISTMAS. *Zen, a Way of Life*, 1962; *A Western Approach to Zen*, 1972.

KAPLEAU, PHILIP. *Three Pillars of Zen*, 1965.

KEATING, H. R. F. *Zen there was Murder* (Fiction), 1960.

LEGGETT, TREVOR. *A First Zen Reader*, 1960.

LINSSEN. *Living Zen*. Trans. from French, 1958.

MIURA AND SASAKI. *The Zen Koan*, 1965.

SCHLOEGL, IRMGARD. *The Wisdom of the Zen Masters*, 1975; *The Record of Rinzai*. Trans. from Chinese, 1975.

SENZAKI and McCANDLESS. *Buddhism and Zen*, 1953.

SHIBAYAMA, ZENKEI. *Zen Comments on the Mumonkan*, 1974.

SUZUKI, D. T. *The Zen Doctrine of No Mind*, 1949; *Living by Zen*, 1950; *The Field of Zen*, 1969; *What is Zen?* 1971.

SUZUKI, SHUNRYU. *Zen Mind, Beginner's Mind*, 1970.

TREVOR, M. H. *The Ox and his Herdsman*. A Chinese Zen Text, 1969.

WATTS, ALAN. *The Way of Zen*, 1970.

WETERING, J. VAN DE. *A Glimpse of Nothingness*, 1975.

Index

168   ZEN BUDDHISM

Flecker, James Elroy 127
Flow, sense of, in Zen 52, 55, 72–4, 154, 156
Ford, the monks at the 13, 77
Friends, Society of 142

Gabb, W. J. 29, 41, 114, 129, 133, 136, 149–50
Ganto 35
ge 116
Gemmell, William 28
God, Zen attitude to 4, 30, 34–6, 64, 99, 111, 137, 141, 143–5
Goddard, Dwight 29; quoted 71–2, 137, 140
Goethe 128
Goose and the bottle, the 12, 79, 129, 149
Gould, Gerald 157
'Gradual' school of Zen 25, 111–13
Guénon, Réné 35

Haiku, 3, 104, 117–19, 129, 130–4
Hakuin 84*n*
Harrison, E. J. 28
Hinayana, 18, 33, 39–40, 138, *see also* Thera Vada
Hojo 26
Holmes, Edmond 97
Hon-Do, 64, 98
Howe, E. Graham 73, 139
hsin (soul) 50ff.
Huang Po 95, 112
Huang Po Doctrine of Universal Mind 29, 48, 93, 155
Hui-ke 24
Hui-neng 1, 3, 23, 25–6, 49–50, 52, 81–2, 84, 112
Humility 65, 122–3
Hung-jen 25
Huxley, Aldous, quoted 4–5, 7, 41, 44, 102–3, 107, 141
Hyakujo 26, 64, 95

Ignorance 1, 17, 75, 154
Images, Zen attitude to 50, 72
Ingen 26
innen 95, 97, 100, 147
Intellect, limitations of the 2–6, 8, 11–13, 34, 100, 104, 141, 154–5

Intuition, development of 6–8, 13–14, 136–7, 147, 158–60; fruits of 15; nature of 2, 7, 14; *versus* Intellect 2–4, 8, 11–13, 15, 34, 100, 104, 120
Isan 102

James, William 94, 108
Japan, art of 59–62; Zen in, 18, 24, 26–7, 59–66, 137
Ji 39, 78–9, 104–5, 127
Jijimuge 12, 35, 39, 78–9, 104–6, 122, 125–6, 149, 154
Jimyo 46
Jiriki (self-power) 37–8, 142
Jiu-Jitsu 61, 147
Jodo Buddhism 26, 37
Johnston, R. F., quoted 40, 138
Joshu 8, 50, 69, 71, 93
Judo 15, 61, 147, 150
Jung, Dr. C. G. 7–8, 89–91, 114, 120, 136, 139, 142, 145–6; quotations from his:
    Essays on Contemporary Events 58
    Psychology and Religion 31
    Secret of the Golden Flower 3, 46, 74, 78, 146–7, 152
Jyoshu 50

Kaiten, Nukariya 28, 33, 44, 48
Kamakura 26, 28–9, 59–60
Karma 15, 37, 42, 54, 63, 87, 101, 108, 116, 139, 141, 155
Kegon School of Buddhism 12, 20, 26, 34, 39, 78, 104–5
Kendo 61
Keyserling, Count 16, 58, 120
Kierkegaard 103
Kipling, Rudyard 14
koan, 10, 26, 33–4, 63–4, 81, 84–92, pass., 93–4, 98, 100, 103, 113, 115, 122, 136, 155
Koizumi, G. 147
Korea 18, 29, 137
Kumarajiva 20
Kwannon Sutra 48
Kyorai 130
Kyoto 26, 38, 60, 63, 110, 116
Kyozen 102

'Labelling' with epithets 14–15, 122, 147

Also published in Mandala

MAGIC AND MYSTERY IN TIBET

Alexandra David-Neel

Alexandra David-Neel studied at the Sorbonne under Professor Foucaux a noted Sanskrit and Tibetan scholar.

She spent many years in the East and especially in Tibet, a closed, awesome, icy and mysterious world. *Magic and Mystery in Tibet* records her fascinating travels and discoveries she experienced in this forbidden country. One of the most distinguished of women explorers, the author brings a commonsense and sceptical eye to the practices and beliefs of the magicians and mystic masters of this ancient dreamland – Tibet.

Amongst the strange events she describes here are how Tibetan mystics can live naked in zero temperatures; how they can run incredible distances without rest, food or drink; how they utilise telepathy and how they appear to defy gravity.

'Precisely the person to explore Tibet . . . absolutely fearless. Her accounts of Tibetan religious ceremonies and beliefs are the fullest and best we have.'
The New Yorker

THE SHORTEST JOURNEY

Philippa Pullar

Most of us live in a terrible muddle. Where are we going? What do we want? Apart from some vague theory of happiness, we have no idea. In terms of Western philosophy, Philippa Pullar seemed to be liberated. Her books were acknowledged. She lived a jet-set life, yet in order to communicate with her friends she had to anaesthetise herself with quantities of alcohol – to such an extent that, among other shattering and riotous experiences, she found herself in bed with the conductor of the last bus home.

The Shortest Journey is the story of her search for something more. In a quest for meaning she made three journeys to India, visiting the ashrams of several well-known gurus. Her introduction came at Allahabad at the Kumbh Mela, the oldest and largest religious fair in the world attracting hundreds of ascetics, some of them naked, who rarely discend from their retreats in the Himalayas. The mere sight of these Sadhus in spectacular procession to their ritual bathing in the Ganges, with elephants, carved wood chariots, conch horns and drums, is believed to cleanse the onlooker of sin.

'Extraordinary travels through a landscape as densely populated with sages and mages as those medieval paintings where every cave, boulder and tree stump sprouts its hermits ... a gripping read.'
Hilary Spurling, The Observer

'Funny, perceptive, mind-churning and hugely readable'.
Basil Boothroyd, The Times

SHAMANS, MYSTICS AND DOCTORS

Sudhir Kakar

Shamans, Mystics and Doctors is a fascinating account of how the ancient healing traditions of India – the rituals of shamans, the teachings of gurus and the precepts of the Ayurveda school of medicine – diagnose and treat emotional disorder.

Sudhir Kakar takes us into a world of Islamic mosques and Hindu temples, of huge gatherings and small, dingy consultation rooms. Drawing on three years research in India and his own psychoanalytic training he reveals a world where patients and healers blame evil spirits for emotional disturbances; where dreams and symptoms are interpreted in terms of deities and legends; where trances are induced to bring out and resolve conflicts of repressed anger, lust and envy and where diet, exercise and conduct are seen as essential to the preservation of a healthy mind and body.

'Sudhir Kakar is concerned with healing, and particularly with the healing of mental and psychosomatic disorders, as practised by a variety of traditional healers in India ... a valuable introduction to some of the many forms of traditional healing in India. It is timely because some teachers of Western medicine have made infections and biochemical disorders the paradigms for every form of illness.'

Nature

I CHING

The Book of Change

Translated by John Blofeld

For 3,000 years *The Book of Change* or *I Ching* has been a guide to prediction of the future. Written before 1000 BC it is the essence of Chinese wisdom. Confucius said that if he had fifty years to live he would devote them to study of the *I Ching*. The authors consider 'change' the most potent force in the universe, but they based their predictions on the observation of Nature and human behaviour. Recently more and more people in the West have become aware of the fascination of the *I Ching*. It is a remarkable combination of mathematical ingenuity and psychological intuition. And when it comes to prediction, it can be uncannily prophetic and is unfailingly intriguing.

STUDIES IN ZEN

D. T. Suzuki

D. T. Suzuki contributes a gentle and profound exposition of the differences between Western and Eastern thought, posing Western intellectualism and materialism against the Eastern concept of acceptance as a basis of the 'whole man'.

D. T. Suzuki, late Professor of Buddhist Philosophy at Otani University, Kyoto, was born in 1869 and died in 1960. He was probably the greatest authority on Buddhist philosophy and Zen Buddhism. His major works in English on the subject of Buddhism number a dozen or more, and he wrote many others in Japanese. Dr Suzuki wrote with authority as he had not only studied original works in Sanskrit, Pali, Chinese and Japanese, but had an up-to-date knowledge of Western thought in German and French as well as in English which he spoke and wrote fluently.

A WESTERN APPROACH TO ZEN

Christmas Humphreys

Buddhism has been known in the West for seventy years. One of the foremost figures in Western Buddhism, Christmas Humphreys, explores in this book the future of Zen in the West and explains how serious students can learn the wisdom of Zen, without the benefit of long years in Zen monasteries. Of the many forms of Buddhism, the Zen School of Japan alone is concerned with a direct, immediate 'breakthrough' into the vast expansion of consciousness which is Enlightenment. Christmas Humphreys advocates deep study of the Buddha's teaching, some meditation and only then a course of mind control and development as preparation for the awakening of the Wisdom-Compassion dormant within.

Available in Mandala

MAGIC AND MYSTERY IN TIBET *Alexandra David-Neel*	£4.95 ☐
THE SHORTEST JOURNEY *Philippa Pullar*	£4.95 ☐
SHAMANS, MYSTICS AND DOCTORS *Sudhir Kakar*	£3.95 ☐
I CHING *John Blofeld*	£4.95 ☐
STUDIES IN ZEN *D. T. Suzuki*	£2.95 ☐
A WESTERN APPROACH TO ZEN *Christmas Humphreys*	£4.95 ☐

All these books are available at your local bookshop or newsagent, or can be ordered direct by post. Just tick the titles you want and fill in the form below

Name ....

Address ....

....

....

Write to Unwin Cash Sales, PO Box 11, Falmouth, Cornwall TR10 9EN.

Please enclose remittance to the value of the cover price plus:

UK: 60p for the first book plus 25p for the second book, thereafter 15p for each additional book ordered to a maximum charge of £1.90.

BFPO: 60p for the first book plus 25p for the second book and 15p for the next 7 books and thereafter 9p per book.

OVERSEAS INCLUDING EIRE: £1.25 for the first book plus 75p for the second book and 28p for each additional book.

Unwin Paperbacks reserve the right to show new retail prices on covers, which may differ from those previously advertised in the text or elsewhere. Postage rates are also subject to revision.